HAMLYN ALL COLOUR BOOK OF
SUPER MACHINES

HAMLYN ALL COLOUR BOOK OF

SUPER MACHINES

HAMLYN

Author: Peter Marriott
Art Director: Brenda Morrison
Designer: Ross George
Production Assistant: Craig Chubb

Published 1986 by
Hamlyn Publishing,
A division of The Hamlyn Publishing Group Limited,
Bridge House, London Road, Twickenham, Middlesex, England.

© Marshall Cavendish Limited 1986

ISBN 0 600 31125 2

Typeset in Rockwell by Quadraset Limited

Printed and bound in Spain
by ARTES GRAFICAS TOLEDO, S.A.
D.L. TO .-931 - 1986

CONTENTS

INTRODUCTION

Efficient use of tools gave Man an advantage over the remainder of the animal kingdom. As Man progressed the tools he used became ever more sophisticated. Tools were used to hunt and kill animals, to process the carcasses, to start fires, plant seeds and tend crops.

The tools became more complicated and evolved into the first machines. The plough and the wheeled cart revolutionized the social organization of Man and started to change the face of the Earth. Machines improved and became more sophisticated.

By the end of the 18th century machines complicated and sophisticated enough to earn the title Supermachine began to appear. The stationary steam engine which helped to power the industrial

Below: Transrapid-06 is a German train run on magnetic levitation. A true Supermachine, it has reached speeds in excess of 320 km/h (200 mph) in tests.

revolution—the first major upheaval in human society for centuries, which brought about a major reshaping of the world—qualifies as one of the first ever Supermachines.

The 20th century has seen the development of an enormous number of Supermachines. Each is fantastic in itself and together they have changed our society.

Supermachines challenge our views of the world.

Today we readily accept motor vehicles, railways and aircraft. Nuclear powered submarines and space probes, tunnel boring machines and robots could not have existed a few years ago.

This book looks at the power and performance at the forefront of present technology and tries to indicate possible directions of future development.

Below left: High-powered motorbikes are the essence of speed and excitement. On these two-wheeled Supermachines treadless tyres give maximum road contact.

Below: Supermachines have made space exploration possible. Here, the Shuttle is seen only moments after take off.

CHAPTER 1

LAND MACHINES

Private and public transport is currently undergoing a revolution in design. Ordinary family saloons and motorcycles are being designed with extra features of safety and comfort in mind, as well as efficient engine performance and economy, and pollution controls. Public vehicles are being redesigned to meet the demands of today's busy world: fire engines to cope with bigger fires in higher buildings; and city buses to transport people efficiently and economically around urban centres.
Farming is also being revolutionized with modern tractors and combine harvesters. Military design, too, is becoming increasingly sophisticated as shown by modern tanks and their weaponry.

Today's fast, elegant Porsche 959 has been developed following years of research and experiment with racing models. Speed and economy, comfort and safety are all combined in this modern luxury sports car. Cars of the future will be operated by computer, with radar for automatic speed control and sonar to warn of obstacles behind.

CARS

The car of the future will recognize your voice. As soon as you get into the car, it will tell you to fasten your safety belt, close the door, insert the ignition key and release the hand brake. Then it may ask you where you wish to go; you will enter the information on the computer by giving north-south, east-west directions, and the computer takes it from there. There will be very little to do, except perhaps steer and choose your speed, although the computer can carry out these procedures as well.

It will also automatically control the windscreen wipers, select the best mixture of fuel and air for the engine and dip the headlights to oncoming traffic. Radar will lead the car ahead on fully automatic cruise control and sonar will reveal obstacles behind.

The car described here does exist. It has been designed by Toyota and is called the EX-11. Other prototypes exist too; experimental cars are not yet mass-produced but, in the years to come, they will be. The EX-11 has a sleek aerodynamic shape so it offers little resistance to the air it moves through. Its body is made of light strong fibre glass. The usual hydraulic-controlled transmission system is replaced by solenoid valves, which, under instruction from the car's central computer, regulate fuel, engine and gears automatically.

People want powerful cars that use little petrol. They want comfort, good suspension, and safety features, such as belts and shock-absorbing bumpers. Most of all, they want their cars to look good, perform well and be mechanically sound.

Motor engineers are continually making improvements in car design, and with advances in technology, the computer-controlled car of the future is not too far away. The main areas in which a car can be improved are in its engine and transmission, its

Two very different looking sports racing cars competing in the Le Mans 24-hour race: *left*, **a Chevrolet Corvette and** *right*, **a Porsche 917.**

shape and weight, and its tyres. Many of these developments come from racing cars whose new designs are tested on the Grand Prix circuits of the world under the most extreme conditions of speed and endurance. If the racing car design is good, it is adapted to the private family saloon.

The petrol-powered internal combustion engine has been used

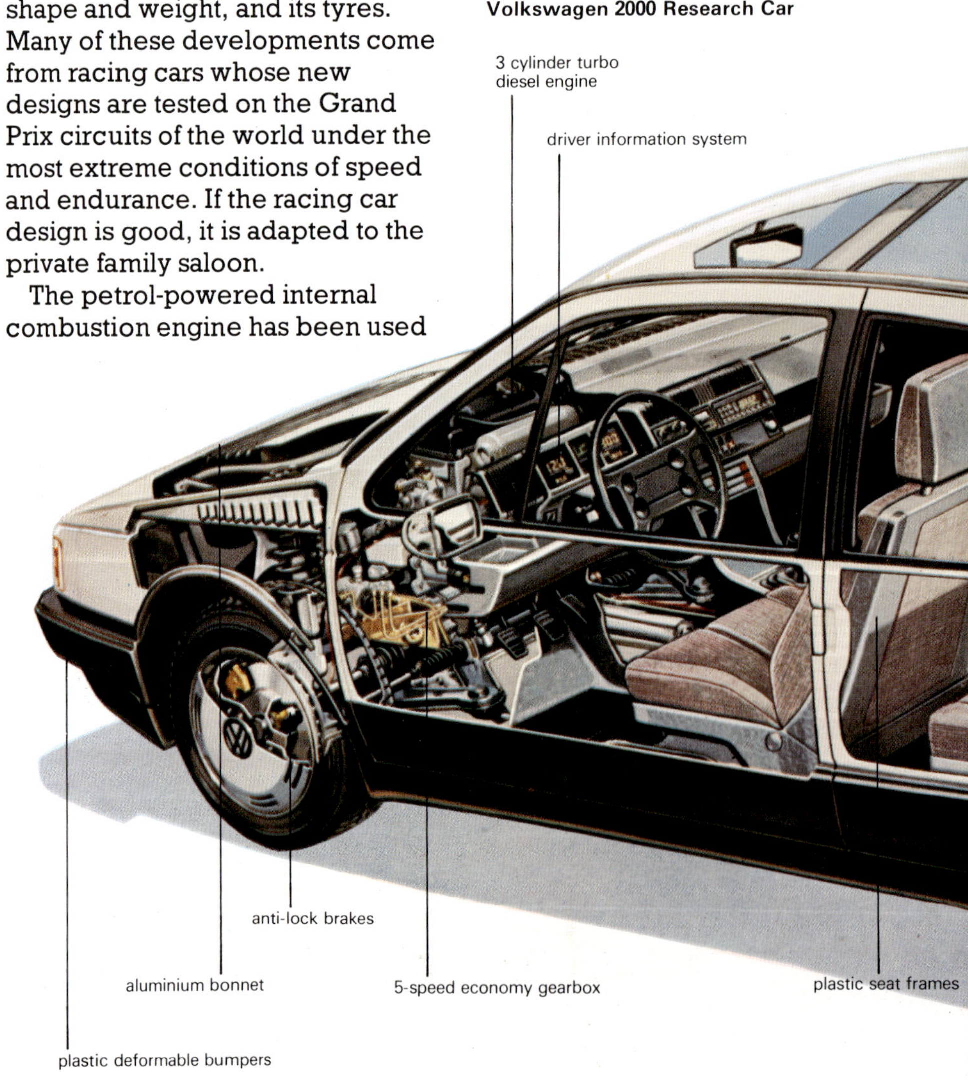

since the 1880s when it was fitted in cars designed by the Germans, Karl Benz and Gottlieb Daimler. Their engines produced ½–1½ horsepower (0.35 to 1.12 kw) and ran at 16 km/h (10 mph)—a long way from the speedy Formula 1 racing car of today.

The performance of the engine has been improved by lowering the speed at which it spins (its revolutions per minute, rpm) and increasing the efficiency of the gears so that savings in fuel are made with no loss in engine power. Other economies have been made, such as using 'lean' mixtures (adding more air to the fuel-air mixture ignited in the combustion chamber). By compressing the mixture more in the cylinders, greater use is made of the fuel.

Electronic systems have been designed to detect if the mixture is too lean, to warn if the engine is about to 'pink' or misfire, and to correct the balance of the mixture. The five-speed gearbox will soon be the norm in cars, just as the four-speed gearbox replaced the three-speed in the 1950s. With all these improvements, the engine of the future will be some 30% more economical. Other engine designs being looked at are the gas turbine engine, like that of an aircraft, and a modified diesel engine which would have spark plugs and a lower compression ratio.

By changing the shape of the car and its weight, further economies can be made. Air resistance, or drag, on the body of a car means that a lot of engine power is being wasted in moving forward. Body shapes are now becoming more sleek and aerodynamic, therefore decreasing drag. The heavier a car is, the more power is needed to move it. Cars are usually made of welded steel panels, but steel is heavy, it rusts and is expensive. New designs have a steel frame only, and the body panels are made of lighter, strong materials, such as plastic reinforced with glass fibre. Aluminium is being used increasingly for radiators, to replace heavy copper wiring in the car's electrical system, and to make engine blocks, gearboxes and axles.

Racing cars are low and wide for speed. They are made of light fibre glass. The driver lies back in the driving seat and this decreases wind drag. Airfoils at the front and rear are angled so that the air pressure pushes the car towards the ground. The powerful engine can have up to 12 cyclinders with 4 valves per cylinder for better fuel injection. All the parts of the car that get hot—the air vents, intakes and radiators—are large and placed so that they are well exposed to the air for cooling. Large air scoops on the wheels cool the disc brakes. The tyres are wide and often smaller at the front to lower drag and larger at the rear for better road holding. They are tubeless and set at a low pressure to avoid blow-outs. In dry conditions, tyres with no treads are used to give maximum contact with the road.

Many different 'formulas' exist for racing cars. The Formula Vee car was introduced in 1961 with a tuned Volkswagen Beetle engine. Emerson Fittipaldi, twice World Formula 1 Champion, raced this car in Brazil before taking the European Grand Prix circuits by storm. There are Formula Fords and Renaults, with 4-cylinder engines and a simple tubular chassis. There are also Super versions of these models, with larger engines. All these different Formula racing cars contribute to the design of the modern private car.

The Volkswagen Auto 2000 is a prototype for testing new designs. A turbo-charged three-cylinder diesel engine gives a fuel consumption of 3.3 litres/100 km (71 miles/gallon). The car has plastic body and wheels.

Left: The Honda TLR 250 trials bike is a lightweight and well balanced machine that is ideally suited for use on rough terrain.

Bottom right: Banking into a tight corner, these racing motorcyclists know the limits of their machines. Treadless tyres are often used.

An acceleration rate of up to 192 km/h (120 mph) in 12 seconds—this is what modern superbikes can achieve. The Japanese lead the market with models such as the Honda CBX, Suzuki GSX1100 and Kawasaki Z1300.

All this power has been squeezed out of a 4-stoke, multi-cylinder engine with overhead camshaft. Years of research have gone into developing the superbike's engine to make it run faster and therefore give more power. Improvements have been made in the valves (they let fuel into the cylinders and exhaust gases out) and in the piston's weight and speed.

Single cylinder bikes used to be the standard engine design. But now, engines with several cylinders, like cars, with four valves per cylinder have been developed. The Kawasaki Z1300 with its 6-cylinder engine has an impressive total of 24 valves. With engines as powerful as this, the Japanese racing bikes can reach speeds over 300 km/h (186 mph).

The fastest road bike in the world is the Honda V65 Magna, with a speed of 278 km/h (173 mph). It has a 4-cylinder, 16-valve engine with an output of 115 horsepower.

Another major design feature of modern bikes is the position of the camshaft (2 cams in the case of the larger models) above the engine. It is directly in contact with the valves. Previously, it was placed below the engine and connected to the valves by a series of pushrods and rockers. By positioning the camshaft above, all this apparatus is unnecessary and therefore the engine is considerably lighter. The pistons have been made shorter and lighter, and they have a shorter stroke. All these design changes had to be made together and the result is a very powerful and efficient engine, which is also surprisingly quiet and smooth.

There have been improvements, too, in throttle controls and in getting the fuel-air mixture to the engine. Racing bikes such as the Kawasaki Z1000 have a fuel injection system similar to that of a car. But unlike a car, with its mechanical ignition system, motorbikes have had an electronically controlled ignition system for years. One type uses a beam of light to activate a photocell which then sparks the plugs.

Brakes on bikes have also been improved, with hydraulically operated disc brakes now fitted on most models. These make the bike much safer.

But a continuing problem for bike designers is the instability of the machine at high speed and on corners. This may be due to the design of the motorbike itself. Although the engine may have become larger and more powerful, the motorbike's frame has not changed in years. It is still an upside-down V shape with wheels front and back, and the steering column at the point of the V. The whole bike is said to have a 'high centre of gravity', with the rider sitting in the centre, high above the gearbox. His body is upright and this causes air resistance or drag on driver and bike. More power is needed to overcome this drag.

Weight distribution is another problem. The heavy wide

Below: A motorcycle cop with a difference. He is riding the Quasar bike, with a top speed of 160 km/h (100 mph). The light fibreglass body is aerodynamically shaped. The rider sits well back, lowering the centre of gravity, which makes the bike more stable at speed and on tight corners. The bike weighs only 317 kg (700 lbs).

engines of the powerful Japanese superbikes put more weight at the front of the machine and may make the bike unstable at speed and while turning corners.

The front forks form part of the bike's suspension. When the bike brakes heavily, the front forks are compressed and this can also make it unstable.

Designers have come up with a whole new concept for building the bike frame. The design has been developed in Britain and is called the Quasar. Two people can sit in it and it may be the answer to combining speed with stability and safety. The frame of the Quasar is in the form of a rectangle, made from light metal alloy tubes. The bike is enclosed to the front and rear in a fibreglass body with a windscreen and roof. The body is an aerodynamic shape and there is little drag on it. The sides are open. The rider sits in a seat to the rear of the bike, his feet well in front of him. This design changes the centre of gravity towards the rear. The engine in the front provides 40 horsepower and a top speed of

160 km/h (100 mph). The Quasar is very manoeuvrable and stable on corners and at speed. Since it looks so different to the traditional big bikes, people may not accept it immediately.

Another new design is the Difazio centre-hub motorcycle. The front forks are horizontal and are joined by an axle running through the centre of the wheel. This axle is secured by a kingpin at the centre. The design allows the Difazio to go around corners with great stability and to handle well at high speeds. The front of the bike is covered with a streamlined body made of light plastic reinforced with glass fibre, and carrying a windscreen. The Difazio is more powerful than the Quasar. Both these new designs may be the bikes of the future. The Difazio is like all of the radical approaches to motorcycle design, in that one of the main objectives is to eliminate the telescopic front forks. This is a weak link in all of the conventional designs because it alters the distance between the wheels as they travel over lumps in the ground and causes instability.

TRUCKS

Heavy goods trucks are the modern workhorses of the motorways. They can pick up cargo in huge metal containers from the docks or drive straight off a Ro-Ro (Roll-on, Roll-off) ferry already laden with tonnes of cargo and go directly to their destination overland.

There are many types of commercial trucks, specialized for different jobs, including luxury coach-type trucks for transporting valuable show-jumping horses, six at a time, to and from events. There are great articulated trucks that follow the Grand Prix circuits of the world, their trailers equipped as workshops with thousands of pounds worth of spare parts, engines, gearboxes and oil. There are trucks that pull trailers fitted out as mobile studios for on-site radio or television broadcasts.

There are also monster-sized breakdown trucks, called 'wreckers', with specialized cranes and winches for rescuing other commercial vehicles. And there are even 'road trains', made up of trucks pulling three or four 'carriages' or containers over vast distances, transporting mixed cargoes.

All modern commercial trucks run on diesel fuel for economy. Long-distance vehicles are also turbocharged, which makes them more efficient on fuel and gives them more power. The turbo unit is driven by a small turbine, which is a fan-like device powered by the engine's exhaust gases. The turbine is connected to a compressor which forces the air, along with the fuel, under pressure into the cylinders. This extra air allows the fuel to be burnt more efficiently and so provides more power to the engine for the same amount of fuel. This simple method of recovering energy from the hot exhaust gases of the engine was pioneered by Volvo, the Swedish truck manufacturers, over 50 years ago. They claim that the power output of the engine is increased by 50%.

About 10% of fuel is also saved.

The size of a truck's engine varies, depending on the job it has to do. Usually it is a six-cylinder engine with a power of between 180 and 350 kw (240 and 470 hp). The engine has to be carefully matched with the truck's gearbox and driving axles. If it is not, up to 25% more fuel can be consumed, making it very uneconomical. The engine and the whole transmission system must therefore act as an efficient unit.

There are as many as 16 speeds in truck gearboxes, with closely spaced ratios. This allows the driver to keep the engine spinning within its most efficient speed range. This number of gears is achieved with half-gears between the normal gears. Most European and Scandinavian trucks have manual gearboxes with synchromesh transmission. American trucks are usually fully automatic.

The backbone of any truck is its chassis. Trucks up to 24 tonnes in weight are built as a one-piece chassis, running on two or three axles. Heavier trucks are built as two units: a tractor with the engine and cab up front and an articulated trailer behind. The trailer is often

Above: A flat-fronted Roadtrain, pulling a long load of carriages, forges its way along the wide dirt roads of the Australian outback delivering vital cargo to isolated towns.

Right: This powerful truck, fuelled by diesel and given extra thrust by its turbo-charged unit, is an economic way of moving heavy loads over great distances.

made of light GRP (glass reinforced plastic) these days, instead of metal, to save on weight and hence fuel.

The flat-fronted design of many modern trucks is called the forward-control or 'cab-over' layout. Here the driver sits above and to one side of the engine. This saves space since the cab can occupy as little as 1.22 m (4 ft) of the truck's length. This is important in some countries since the overall length of commercial vehicles which use motorways is restricted by law. The whole cab unit can tilt forward so that the engine can be serviced.

The shape of a truck's body and its trailer is important for the economic running of the engine. Driving into a strong wind can increase the amount of fuel used

by 50%, because the truck has to overcome air resistance. Trucks with a large front area suffer more from drag. At speeds of 70 km/h (less than 45 mph), about one-third of the engine's power is being wasted in overcoming drag. At 90 km/h (56 mph), this is increased to half the engine's output. Much effort and research has gone into finding a design to decrease significantly this waste of energy. For example, Britain's Leyland Vehicles have tested the design of the new T45 Roadtrain truck in the same wind tunnel that was used to test the aerodynamic shape of Concorde. The smallest features are carefully looked at, such as the rear-view mirrors and side windows. The T45 design has reduced drag by about 30%; work is continuing to reduce this further.

The inside of the long-distance commercial trucks, for example those travelling to the Middle East, is like a small apartment, with bunks, a fridge, cooker and washbasin.

The cabin is air-conditioned and insulated so the temperature is contant. Noise level and road vibrations are kept low, at about 71–74 decibels of sound.

Sophisticated electronic equipment is fitted in the cab, to check the electrical system of the truck and to warn of tyre pressures, load shifts, wheel imbalance or brake wear. Microcomputers are now being developed that will give the driver constant readings on engine performance, the best route to take between two points on the map and the average speed for the trip. Already, some trucks have a 'cruise control' setting installed so that the driver can set the truck to move at a pre-determined speed on long, straight stretches of highway.

Safety features in trucks today include lower bumper heights, an energy-absorbing barrier at the rear, and safety skirts around the sides so that cars will not run under a truck in a collision. Some trucks have cameras mounted at the back and a screen in the cab to show obstacles behind. Others have ultra-sonic sensors that bounce sound waves off obstacles which tell the driver if he is too close to them. Trucks are now fitted with power brakes and anti-skid equipment to prevent 'jack-knifing' of the articulated trailer.

BUSES

There is a revolution going on in bus design today. Many new types are already on the roads, others are at the planning stage. This re-think about bus design has been prompted by the great numbers of people travelling in cities every day. Running private cars is very expensive and traffic congestion in city centres leads to delays, air pollution and greater amounts of fuel being used. So the bus is being developed as an efficient economic way of mass transport within cities. The old-fashioned tram and trolley-bus are also making a come-back, but with modern high technology designs.

Already on our roads we see cleaner, faster diesel-run buses, operating in special bus lanes. The double-decker is a familiar sight and allows more people to travel at one time. In the USA, long buses are used which are suitable for the long straight streets of American cities. Articulated buses are used in many European capitals and these can manoeuvre around the narrow winding streets of older cities.

The first tram ran in New York city in 1832. It was a four-wheeled vehicle which ran on a rail set in the road and was pulled along by a horse. By the 1880s, there were over 4830 km (3000 miles) of tramway in the USA and 18,000 horse trams. Electricity provided an easier way of moving the tram. In America and Germany, the idea of attaching a tram to an overhead electric wire via a cable gave birth to the electric tram of today. In Britain, Manchester had electric trams in 1890 and the first electric line opened in London in 1901. Modern systems may have electric cables running in a conduit or drain set into the road surface instead of overhead wires.

THINK ELECTRIC

Electric trams are now popular in many cities of the world. For example, double-decker trams operate along Hong Kong's busy streets. Several units coupled together ferry people around Zurich, Vienna and many other European cities. A tramway system costs one-fifth that of an underground railway system.

Trolleybuses also get their power from overhead electricity cables but, unlike trams, they do not need rails to run on. This makes them much more manoeuvrable than trams. They run on three sets of rubber tyres. The first English trolleybuses operated in Leeds and Bradford in 1911. London followed

in 1931 and by 1952 there was a fleet of 1800 on the road, double-deckers looking much like the modern motor bus but with six wheels.

West Germany is the major developer of new trolleybus designs. Modern versions use a combination of overhead wires and a diesel engine. The trolley-diesel bus can thus go away from the

Below: A moving passenger lounge, this bus takes people directly to the aircraft and lifts them right up to the door. It can carry up to 150 passengers and is a most efficient means of transporting people around airports today.

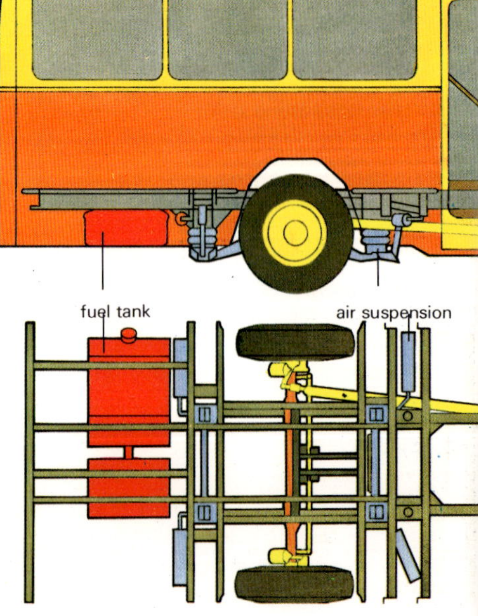

electricity source overhead and power itself by engine in areas of the city where there are no power lines. Another type of trolleybus has batteries for storing some of the overhead electricity and using this stored power for trips in unwired areas. One of the problems with the trolley-battery design is the weight of the batteries. The bus weighs 18 tonnes, with no people aboard, and this is above the legal limit of 10 tonnes.

The next design to be tried is the trolleybus with both diesel power and storage batteries. Acceleration and braking in these modern trolleybuses is controlled electronically and this saves up to 10 per cent on energy. Another way of saving energy, and cutting down on wear and tear, is to use alternating current (AC) in the overhead power lines rather than the conventional direct current (DC).

Special lanes in city traffic have made bus transport more efficient. Paris has the most extensive system of bus lanes in the world —over 110 km (69 miles). A new development is to give buses priority at traffic lights. This works automatically, by special electronic loops in the road and equipment on the bus which together trigger the lights to turn green as the bus approaches. In Sweden, they have developed a system where an auto-pilot control on the bus steers it alongside the bus stop to pick up or let down passengers.

An experimental bus, developed in Britain, has no driver. It is driven over an electronic cable buried in the road which is programmed to steer the bus automatically, to stop it or start it. Coils along the cable are also programmed to make the bus go at different speeds. Such technology could lead to driverless buses in the future, finding their way around narrow streets in city centres guided by computer.

British designers have also developed the idea of a bus-train —a conventional bus that runs on a railway line by means of small guide wheels that lead it along the tracks. It can take to the road again by simply folding up its guide wheels and running on its rubber tyres. In Germany, such bus-trains are already operating very effectively as part of the O-Bahn passenger transport system. They offer great advantages in fuel economy and transport efficiency, and are being further developed by the Daimler-Benz company.

Left: An 18 m (60 ft) long articulated bus carries passengers from plane to terminus at Heathrow Airport, London. It is very manoeuvrable and can make a tight turn in a circle of only 22 m (72 ft) diameter.
Below: The side-view and undercarriage of the bus show its structure.

FIRE ENGINES

Modern fire-fighting depends a lot on the speed and reliability of the fire engine. After the alarm is raised, the vehicle must be on the road within seconds and racing to the scene of the fire. It must have the right equipment aboard for fighting the blaze. Water alone is often not sufficient to put out flames. The men need special clothing and gear to protect themselves. And once on the scene, the fire crews need access to the fire for their bulky vehicles. Coordination with the police and ambulance service is important. Communications with each other and the Fire Brigade headquarters is also vital. Like the crews of lifeboats, firemen face terrible dangers and we owe much to their dedication and bravery. Without their skills and courage, the best equipment in the world would be useless.

Computers are being increasingly used today in Fire Brigade stations. Alarm calls are received in a central control area and then the appropriate fire stations are alerted. Information is coordinated on the type of fire, special dangers involved (such as chemicals or petrol) or special equipment needed and this is relayed to the fire stations and, by radio, to the vehicles en route to the scene. Some modern fire engines have their own computer terminal installed so that they have a complete, up-to-date print-out on the fire as they travel.

A modern fire engine can be on the road in 30–60 seconds. It is a 6-wheeled vehicle with a turbo-charged diesel engine. This provides 450–500 horsepower and drives the vehicle at a speed of 100 km/h (60 mph). The acceleration rate can be 0–80 km/h (0–50 mph) in just 35 seconds. A fire engine weighs some 18 tonnes, though some can be up to 30 tonnes, with a height of 4 m (13 ft).

Attachments for fire-fighting are carried on the vehicle. There is an aerial platform at the end of a long, articulated steel ladder, called a boom. Firemen climb onto the platform and are raised up to the level of the fire. This is particularly important these days with so many multi-storey offices and tower blocks of flats. The boom is set on a turntable on top of the fire engine so it can be swung in any direction during fire-fighting. The great elbow-like joint of the boom allows it to get up and over obstacles if necessary. Such booms can reach a height of 28 m (92 ft). The boom is operated by hydraulic pressure and can manoeuvre horizontally, vertically, diagonally or even through a complete 360° circle.

Different extinguishers are needed for different types of fire. Water will quench most flames and can be directed through powerful jet hoses, reeled out from the fire engine. Carbon dioxide gas or dry powders are useful for electrical fires or where water or foam would damage valuable items such as paintings or manuscripts. With flammable liquids, such as oil or petrol, foam is best and is discharged from hoses or a cannon mounted on top of the fire engine. The nozzle on the cannon can be changed to give a wide spray or a powerful concentrated jet. The whole cannon revolves on a turntable so it can be directed anywhere it is needed.

A modern airport fire engine, such as the Rosenbauer Simba model, has steel tanks to carry 9000 litres (almost 2000 gallons) of water and 1000 l (220 gals) of foam. These can be mixed and discharged at a rate of 6300 l (1386 gals) per minutes, over a range of 60 m (200 ft). A separate 256 hp diesel engine pumps the water from its tank through hoses. The foam cannon mounted on the roof can be used

Below: A small airport fire engine rushes to the scene of the blaze, a fireman in position behind the powerful foam cannon. Speed is of the essence when flammable materials are involved.

A cut-away of a fire engine shows the turbo-charged diesel engine and the propeller-shaft drive of the 6-wheeled chassis. Water and foam tanks are in the middle, articulated boom at the back and foam cannon at the front. The vehicle is economic and efficient.

when the vehicle is on the move, aiming the foam at the flames as the fire is circled.

Each fire engine carries a crew of three to four men. There is a spacious cabin and room behind for changing into protective gear while the vehicle is rushing to the scene. There is also an air-conditioned unit in all fire engines, installed as standard. Protective clothing for firemen is essential. Helmets and oil skins are standard. Aluminium asbestos suits protect them if they

have to go into the heart of a blaze, such as at an aircrash, to rescue victims. These suits were originally developed for RAF ground crews. Breathing apparatus may be needed where there are poisonous fumes and heavy smoke in a building. Compressed air (like divers use) in light, fire-resistant tanks is carried. The apparatus is designed so that the pressure inside the face mask is slightly above atmospheric pressure. This gives a snug fit on the face and

stops poisonous fumes getting in if the mask slips during work.

A recent development in fire-fighting is transporting special units, called pods, to the scene of a fire which may take several days to extinguish. These pods carry specialized equipment such as mobile compressors, breathing apparatus, decontamination units, turntable ladders, hydraulic platforms and even canteen units. They can be trailed to the scene, then detached and left on site.

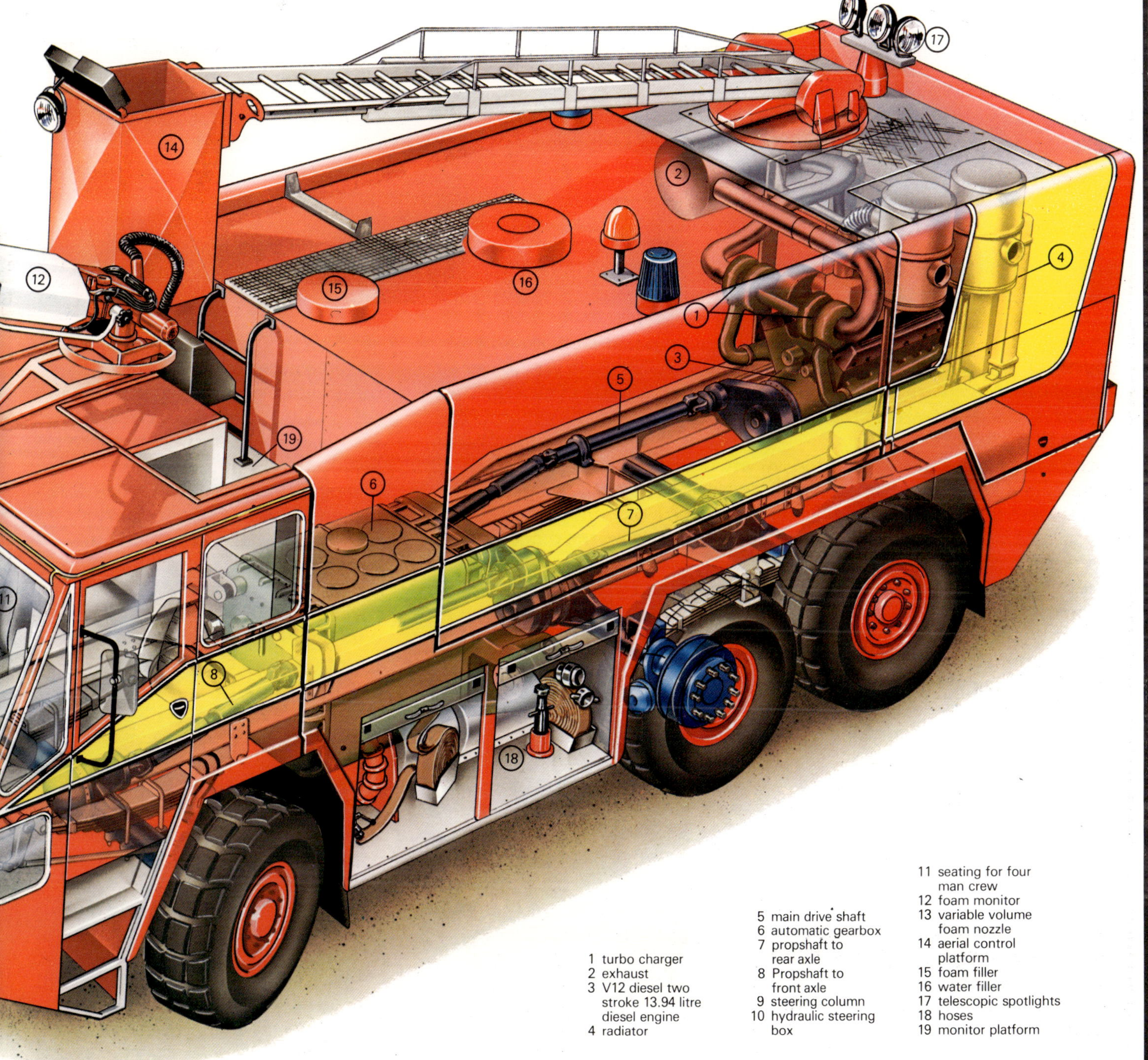

OVER ALL TERRAIN

An ordinary family saloon, a nippy sports car or even a sturdy station-wagon cannot go very far off the smooth surface of a tarmac road. These cars are not built for tough-going over difficult terrain. Firstly, they are not high enough off the ground and the chassis and delicate transmission parts would get damaged bumping over rough ground. It would also be very uncomfortable since their suspension is not intended for such punishment.

A vehicle has to be specially designed to combat such conditions. There are several types, known as all-terrain vehicles (ATVs). In recent years, they have been designed for military use, scientific expeditions and simply for fun—for the adventurous to explore the most inaccessible parts of the world. Other ATVs are working commercial vehicles, designed to carry heavy loads of vital cargo over harsh lands, such as the frozen wastes of Canada or the USSR, or through the tropical swamps of South America.

The Jeep and Land Rover are familiar ATVs. Both are designed to tackle all kinds of terrain. They are built high off the ground. The chassis, wheel axles and exhaust are hoisted high between the wheels, well out of harm's way. They have big wheels and special ribbed tread on the thick rubber tyres to give a large surface area for gripping the ground. (The larger the surface area, the better the traction, as seen in tracked vehicles such as tanks and tractors which move easily over soft ground.) There are two gearboxes: one is a normal gearbox and the second is a 'transfer' gearbox. Effectively, this gives the vehicle more low gears and therefore more pulling-power. When a Jeep is in low transfer gear, the engine develops peak power even though the vehicle is moving at very low speeds, less than walking pace in fact. Thus, Jeeps can climb steep slopes or travel through thick mud or snow.

Jeeps and Land Rovers do not get stuck on slippery slopes or bogged down in oozing mud because they have a drive differential system which can be locked. The differential, which is usually on the drive axle, is a system of gearing which allows one wheel to move faster than the other. This is essential if the vehicle is to be able to turn a corner without skidding because the outer wheel has to cover a greater distance and, therefore, move faster. However, on slippery ground this can mean that one wheel spins helplessly while the other, which might be able to get a grip and drive the vehicle, is completely stationary. Jeeps and Land Rovers have a system for short-circuiting, or locking, the differential which results in both wheels moving at the same speed. They now have a better chance of getting a grip and driving the vehicle forward. In a four-wheel drive system, the differential on all the wheels locks and the chances of getting stuck are even smaller.

There is no single vehicle that will go over absolutely *all* terrain, especially if water is included as a 'terrain', as it is nowadays. A Jeep

Left: The British Range Rover is a luxury version of the older Land Rover. Just as practical and tough, it can cruise on a motorway, ford a stream and tow a load of 4000 kg (8800 lbs) in style and comfort.

Above: The amphibious Crayford *Cargocat* has 8 balloon tyres which keep it afloat and a light, watertight body. It can deal with soft and rocky ground and climb steep slopes.

or Land Rover can cover most types of ground but it cannot cross a swamp or a wide river. A hovercraft can, however. It can also glide over rapids, run up onto a beach or travel along a dirt track. Riding high on its cushion of air, a hovercraft is an excellent water vehicle and very passable on land so long as it is smooth. But if it encounters rocky ground, steep slopes or wide ditches, the hovercraft comes to a halt.

A design that solves the problems of both water and rough ground is a vehicle that moves on wide, balloon-like tyres. These are so soft that they are not damaged by rocks and other rough obstacles. They roll so gently over soft ground that they hardly make an impression. And they can even keep the vehicle afloat in water. The US *Amphicat* is an ATV with six or eight fat, ribbed, very soft tyres. Each tyre holds air at a pressure of only 1.5 pounds per square inch (psi), one-fifteenth that of a normal tyre. The body is light, weighing only 180 kg (396 lbs), and sealed to make it water-tight, so it can cross rivers buoyed up on its tyres. Low gears allow it to climb

steep slopes and the soft tyres spread out, giving great traction on muddy and loose, sandy ground. The vehicle has two clutches to drive the wheels on either side. When both are engaged, the vehicle moves forward; when one is released, the vehicle changes course. This simple driving system is designed to allow the driver to concentrate on the route ahead. The vehicle is powered by a single

cylinder, two-stoke, air-cooled engine. The only problem with the *Amphicat* is that it cannot carry heavy loads, 220 kg (480 lbs) being the maximum. But as a pleasure vehicle, it is ideal.

Another ATV for pleasure is the powered tricycle, with three wide balloon tyres. This arrangement gives it great stability at low speeds. Automatic transmission makes it simple to drive and it can easily cope with rough terrain. The tyres keep it afloat. It is small and light enough to actually pick up and man-handle out of a difficult spot.

Invaluable for moving over snow and ice, the snow-scooter or skidoo is another light, one-man ATV. No husky dogs pull this motorized sledge. It can haul heavy loads at speeds of 32 km/h (20 mph) per hour, moving on rubber tracks whose wide surface give it traction on the slippery surface. A ski at the front steers it. With simple gearbox and automatic clutches, the driver has ample time to select the best route across the frozen plains. Skidoos are used throughout Canada and Scandinavia, and the USSR has its own version.

Below: The motorized sledge or skidoo moves on rubber tracks steered by a ski, perfect for snow and ice conditions.

TRACTORS

The days of horse-drawn ploughs are gone. Today in place of the horse we have a sophisticated machine designed and perfected by modern engineering technology. This is the modern tractor. The driver sits in a comfortable seat in an air-conditioned cab, maybe listening to music as he works. The turbo-charged engine produces power equal to that of 280 horses, in some cases up to 340 horsepower. Moving at walking pace in one of its 24 gears, the tractor with its attached machinery can do several jobs at the same time, such as hoeing and spraying insecticide.

Today's tractor is a versatile machine. It is powerful, economic and rugged. The engine runs on diesel and burns it more efficiently than petrol, by about 10 per cent. Diesel is also cheaper than petrol. Depending on the size of the tractor and its job, the power from the engine varies from 20 to 280 hp generally. The smallest tractors have 3-cylinder engines and are built to work in confined areas such as orchards or vineyards. They are long and narrow; they are also very manoeuvrable since they have to work between trees or vine plants and often their wheels are covered to prevent them damaging tree roots or branches. The giant tractors that work the vast prairies of North America are much more powerful, up to 340 hp with an 8-cylinder engine. The world's largest tractor is owned by the US Department of Agriculture. It measures 10 m (33 ft) between the wheels and runs on its own permanent pathways. The advantage of being so wide is that the tractor has to make less passes over the field and less ground is wasted by its 22-tonne weight compacting the soil.

The engine of a tractor is not built for speed. It is built for pulling and turning force, called torque. A tractor must be able to pull heavy agricultural machinery, such as a plough or seed sower, all day often

Above: Three pairs of equal-sized wheels with widely spaced treads give great traction to this large American tractor and mounted plough, working an English field. Such machines are monuments of tractor design.

at a snail's pace over hard or soft earth. It has to be reliable to get the job done when the season is right and the weather is fine.

Besides having a powerful engine, a tractor also has a powerful transmission system. The clutch and engine are bolted directly to the gearbox, making a strong backbone down the centre of the vehicle. There may be as many as 24 gears to transmit drive to the wheels. With so many gears, a tractor can combine very low speeds with great pulling power without the wheels slipping.

Like in a Jeep or Land Rover, there are normal gears and 'transfer' gears, which give a much lower range of gears. Thus a tractor can come out of a field where it has been doing drainage work, for example, at less than walking pace and then run down the road at a speed of 30 km/h (19 mph).

Many tractors these days do not have clutches. Instead they have an oil-powered or hydraulic transmission system which gives a continuous range of speeds. They can shift from forward into reverse smoothly, which is useful for loading and forklift work.

Four-wheel drive tractors, where the wheels all move at the same speed, are popular today. They give better traction, or grip, with less chance of slipping. The weight is also spread evenly over the four wheels and the soil is less compacted, which may be very important for certain crops. In Italy, where there are many hilly areas cultivated, almost half the tractors are four-wheel drives. They can work on a slope of 34° to the horizontal. In Britain, most tractors are two-wheel drive. European and American tractors have different sized wheels. European vehicles usually have two small front wheels and a large back pair. This helps steering in small fields. Steering is not so important in the wide open spaces of the prairies. The wheels of US tractors are all the same size, larger diameter wheels for maximum grip over vast areas while loaded with farm machinery.

In heavy wet soil, tracked tractors are used. These run on a caterpillar linked track, like a tank, and this spreads the weight of the vehicle over the ground so it does not sink. It also provides a larger surface area for traction. Tracks are also useful on very hard dry soil where rubber tyres would be quickly worn out.

There are a whole range of farming implements—for ploughing, hoeing, sowing seeds, spraying and harvesting. These can be mounted on a tractor at the front and back. Two machines working at the same time from a single tractor save time and money. Their point of attachment is called the power take-off. They are hitched to the tractor by a hydraulically powered linkage system so that they can be turned at the end of a field, folded up when travelling on the road to the next field or lifted off the ground to the correct height for the job in hand. Different jobs need different heights. Ploughing, for example, needs precise control. The height can be easily adjusted by the driver from his cab by using a hand lever, or electronic switch in the most modern tractors. The system works on oil and valves control the flow of oil to and from the machinery.

By mounting a piece of machinery onto a tractor, it becomes part of the tractor. Its downward force gives the tractor more grip and stability, thus overcoming the resistance of the soil to a machine being pushed or pulled through it. It is this hydraulic system that makes tractors so versatile. It was Harry Ferguson who perfected the system and it is still called the 'Ferguson three-point linkage' system.

KEY
1. 6-cylinder engine
2. 16-speed gearbox
3. 2-speed power take-off
4. Linkage for implements
5. Hydraulic lift

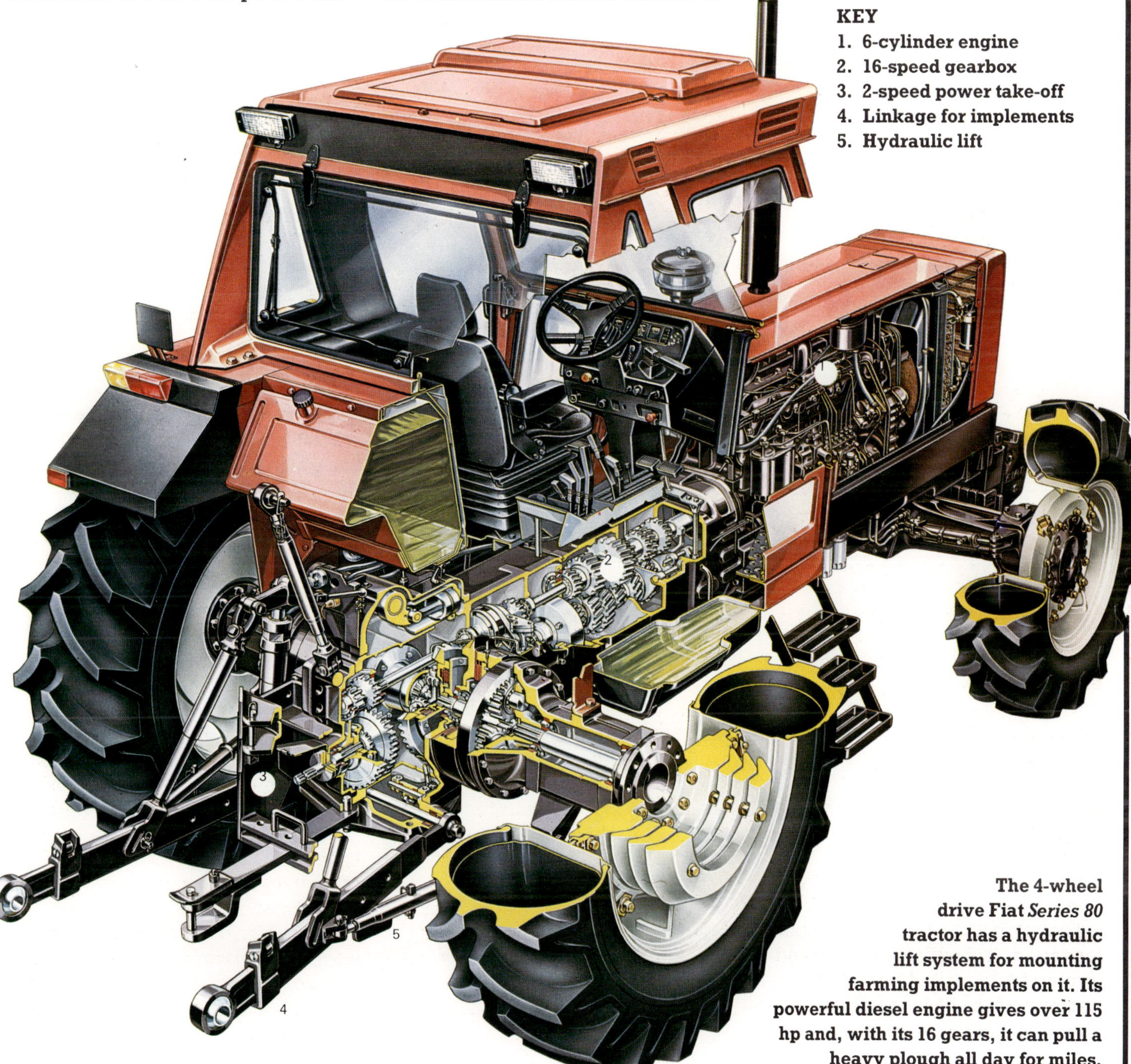

The 4-wheel drive Fiat *Series 80* tractor has a hydraulic lift system for mounting farming implements on it. Its powerful diesel engine gives over 115 hp and, with its 16 gears, it can pull a heavy plough all day for miles.

HARVESTERS

A combine harvester is a giant factory on wheels. A feat of modern engineering technology, it is made up of 35,000 different parts. It moves through a sea of golden wheat, cutting it, threshing or beating the valuable grain out of the cereal's ears and then separating it from the straw. This machine can harvest up to 1.6 hectares (4 acres) in an hour. In Britain, an average acre yields about 2 tonnes of grain; thus in a full working day over 14 tonnes of wheat can be gathered and sent on its way to be made into bread and other commodities.

Giant machines move across the prairies of North America, harvesting the rich crop of cereals. Massive diesel engines drive these combine harvesters, each with a power of 300 hp and a capacity of 10,000 cc. They cut a path 10 m (30 ft) wide and many machines operate together, making light work of the harvest. In Britain and many parts of Europe, smaller harvesters are used, with an average power of 75–90 kw (100–120 hp.) Some do not even have an engine but are mounted on and drawn by tractors. Since the fields and gateways are much smaller and the crops are planted closer together, harvesters cut a narrower path, about 3–6 m (10–12 ft) wide.

The combine harvester is probably the most expensive piece of machinery a farmer owns, perhaps second only to his house in terms of price. It can cost more than £40,000 ($60,000). And this is a great capital outlay for a machine that may lie idle during 11 months of the year, used only at harvest time. But in terms of getting the harvest in at the right time, it is a great labour-saving device. And this is what the farmer wants—speed in gathering the harvest before bad weather spoils it; efficiency in separating the grain from the straw, for this is where the money lies; and economy which is achieved by running the machine on cheap diesel fuel, with one man operating it.

A combine harvester performs its three jobs—cutting, threshing and separating the grains of cereals— very efficiently. Rice, broad beans, peas, poppies, soya beans, Brussels sprouts, apples, strawberries—can also be harvested by machine, although the design of the harvester's parts will vary with the type of crop.

First, as the harvester moves forward, great rotating sails in front gather the crop and pull it towards the cutting blades. It is held steady and cut at ground level, or 'stubble height' as it is called. The blades can cut at a speed of 515 cycles per minute. Cutting height can be adjusted by a hydraulic system

Left: Today, there are even harvesters for picking orchard fruit. Here a row of specially bred apple trees form a hedge along which the machine can move. Rows of flexible 'fingers', in groups of three (a little like a hand), probe the trees, then gently lift and detach the fruit.

under the control of the driver and the whole front of the machine can move up or down. The most recent models of harvester have the cutting height adjusted automatically as the machine moves over uneven ground.

Next, the cut stalks of cereal are passed up to the threshing area by spinning screws, or augers, and an elevator. Here the grain is beaten out of the ears of the crop in a rotating drum. There are rubber 'rasp' bars on the surface of the drum and below it, on a grid called the concave. As the cereal spins around the drum, the rubber bars on both surfaces knock out the grains. The drum can rotate at speeds of 400–1400 rpm depending on its size. The gap between the drum and the concave can also be adjusted by hydraulic power according to the cereal crop being threshed.

Once the grain has been separated from the straw, it falls through a series of sieves and then through a 'winnowing' blast of air. This blows away the chaff (any small pieces of straw, dust and weed seeds). The grain, now in the

bottom of the machine, passes along an auger and up an elevator into the grain tank. This can hold up to 8 tonnes in the large combine harvesters and has to be emptied every 20 minutes. The grain is offloaded down a long chute into a truck which can drive alongside the harvester, moving slowly as the grain fills its tank. The whole operation takes less than two minutes.

The straw that is left in the threshing area of the harvester passes toward the back of the machine along a series of trays, called 'straw walkers'. In some harvesters, the straw is lifted and shaken again here, letting more precious grain fall out and collect in a pan below. After the last walker, the straw falls off the back on to the ground where it may be burnt later in the season, to add potash and other chemicals to the soil as

fertilizer for next year's crop.

In the most modern harvesters, electronic sensors and monitors warn the driver of any problems with the machinery. For example, grain may be lost to the ground through the sieves or from the back of the machine. Or the sieves may be blocked with too much grain, the straw walkers clogged up, or the grain tank may be full.

A major design change has taken place in the threshing area of the harvester in recent years. American engineers have turned the traditional drum and concave apparatus through 90° to stand upright, and fitted it with spiral rasp bars. This new rotary drum seems to separate the grain more gently and more efficiently. Since the cereal spends more time in the thresher, spiralling around its bars, more grain can be extracted, achieving 30% higher yields.

Below: Looking like tanks, a group of giant combines, their grain chutes at the ready, engage in intensive harvesting of the North American prairies.

Above: The Allis Chalmers N6 rotary 'gleaner' makes light work of the harvest, offloading its 6 tonnes of grain in about two minutes.

Left: Harvesting a cereal crop up a 20° slope is now possible with machines that have automatic levelling systems so the threshing drum, sieves and straw walkers do not get clogged up. The only part of the harvester to follow the steep angle of the hillside is the cutting bar.

THE TANK

Tanks were secretly developed by the British and used in World War I to breach the German defences. In the 70 years since then, tanks have developed into formidable battle machines, mobile platforms of guns and firepower. But the tanks of World War I and today's tanks have the same basic features. They run on caterpillar linked tracks which give them grip or traction over rough or soft ground, even through water. They have a turret which revolves in a complete circle. The main gun is mounted at the front and machine- and anti-aircraft guns are placed all round. They carry a crew of three to five men, who get in and out of the tank through hatches which can be sealed. They are encased in heavy steel armour to protect against anti-tank shells.

Basically, a tank consists of a hull or body which rests on the wheeled suspension system of linked tracks and high-energy shock absorbers. Above the hull is the rotating turret. The driver sits inside the hull, with most of the ammunition, the motor and transmission, and the fuel. The turret houses the weapons and some ammunition, the communications equipment and the guidance and control systems for missiles and rockets. Three men work it: the commander, the gunner and the loader or radio operator. In smaller tanks and in the fast reconnaissance vehicles of today, there may be only a crew of three, with two in the turret. Here there is a sighting system for the main gun

with a thermal image unit built in. This 'sees' the heat given off by an enemy tank and produces a picture for the gunner to aim at. Battles can be carried out in dense fog or at night by means of the infra-red night vision system. Laser equipment can find the range of the enemy and pinpoint the position accurately. The tank is fitted with a filtering system to protect the crew against radioactive fallout.

There are four or five types of weapon carried. Guided missiles can home in on their target. Conventional high-speed shells that pierce the armour of a tank are still used, as in World War II. Other shells act by melting the tank's armour or exploding on delayed fuses to create shock waves which shatter the armour. Either way, the result is the same: deadly sharp pieces of steel implode into the tank, flying about its small interior and killing the crew.

Tanks used to run on petrol. In the last war, fuel depots were blown up

Cut-away of a modern main battle tank, the German *Leopard 2* is designed for speed and mobility. Powered by a 4-stroke turbo-charged engine, it travels cross-country at 35 km/h (20 mph). Protected by heavy Chobham armour and a 120 mm main gun, this tank can withstand most attacks.

Fact file . . .

The heaviest tank ever built was an experimental German *Panzer*, weighing 192 tonnes. The design was abandoned in 1945. The most heavily armed tank since 1972 is the Soviet *T72*, with a 125 mm high-velocity main gun. The world's fastest tank is the modern British *Scorpion ARV*, with a top speed of 80 km/h (50 mph).

or captured, or the supply routes to the tanks were cut off. Diesel engines power tanks today, some with turbo-chargers. The latest development is the American gas turbine engine, fitted in its most recent tank, the XM1 MBT. Based on

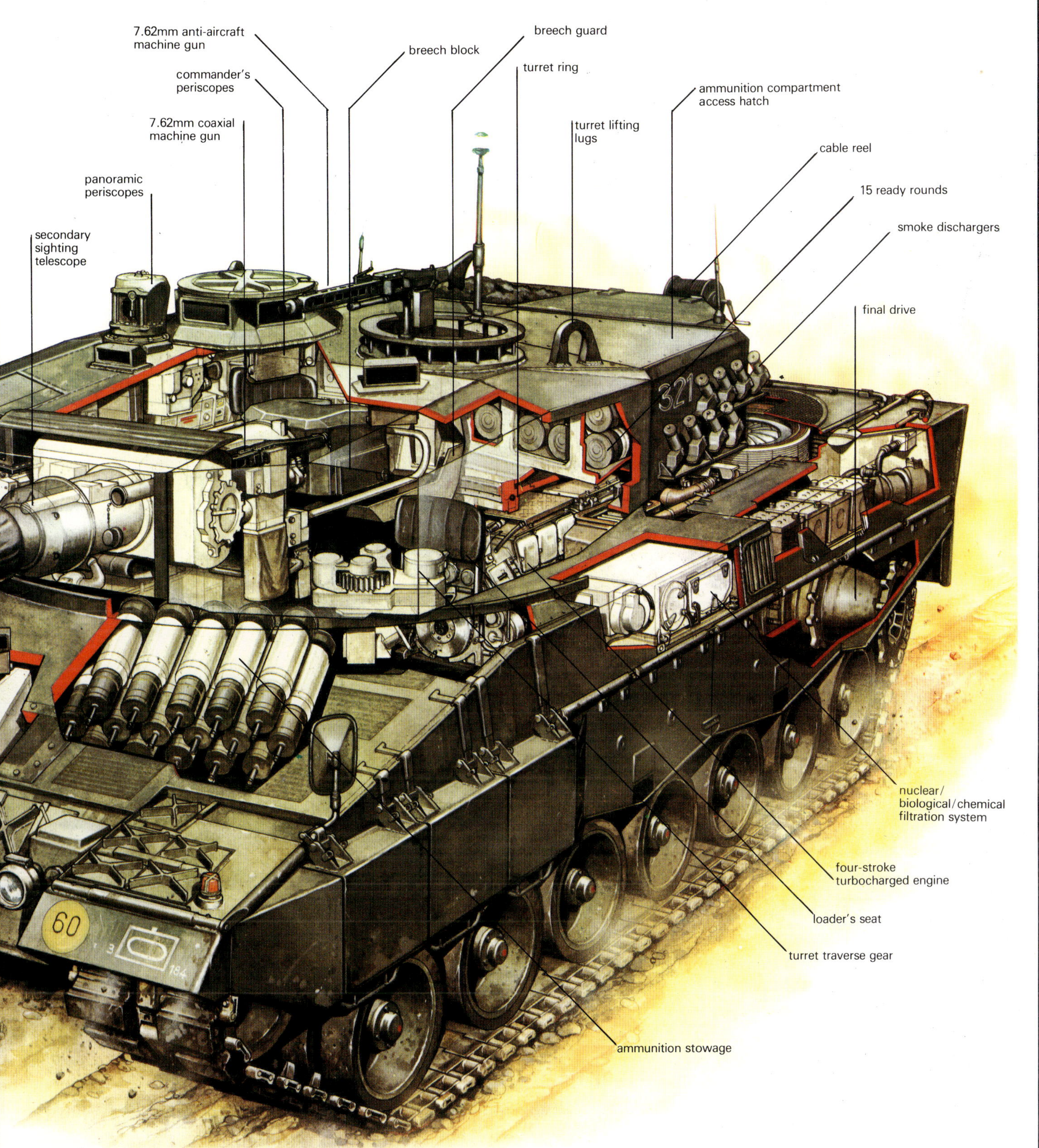

the jet aeroplane's engine, the gas turbines produce 1000 horsepower. The engine can also run on gasoline, diesel or jet fuels, giving a valuable choice in times of war. Light tanks, such as the British *Scorpion* reconnaissance tank, can reach speeds of 80 km/h (50 mph).

Tanks have sloping armoured sides to deflect shells, especially at the front of the hull and turret—the most vulnerable areas. Today, a new type of armour has been designed in Britain called Chobham armour. Its structure is top secret but it is thought to consist of a double thickness of special alloy metal plates, the space between the plates filled with a granular material to absorb or disperse any fragments that a shell will have dislodged.

CHAPTER 2

RAILWAYS

At the beginning of the 19th century the best way of transporting goods was via the network of canals—but this was slow and there was only a limited network. The method of transporting passengers was by horse drawn coach over poor roads —an uncomfortable ride at the best of times.

When the first railway was built, constructed of strong, smooth iron rails, it had no competition as the fastest and most comfortable means of transport.

Rail held this position for many years until improved modern roads were built and cheap airline services began. After some years as a shrinking industry, rail is now growing again with the development of new Supertrains— providing faster and more comfortable services.

The German experimental magnetic levitation train _Transrapid-06_ has reached speeds of over 320 km/h (200 mph) on a test track.

Richard Trevithick produced the first steam locomotive in 1804. By 1830 when George Stephenson produced the *Rocket* locomotive, railways were established as the fastest means of transporting people and goods. An enormous explosion of railway development took place in the remainder of the century and railways were established as the main form of public transport in most developed countries.

Above: The 1938 Mallard *Flying Scotsman* inside the National Railway Museum at York.

Right: A prototype of the Advanced Passenger Train which is designed to travel on existing tracks but has a revolutionary tilting body to increase its ability to travel around corners at high speed.

STEAM ENGINES

The motive power for these railway engines was steam, using coal or wood as fuel. The steam locomotives produced were generally reliable but not particularly clean or efficient. However, development continued to produce better, faster and more efficient locomotives.

The culmination of this development was a group of streamlined, high-speed locomotives which included the famous *Mallard*.

Mallard was designed by Sir Nigel Gresley to pull high-speed passenger trains on the London North Eastern Railways' route between London and Edinburgh. In 1938 *Mallard* achieved a speed of 203 km/h (126 mph) pulling a light train of carriages, a world record for steam locomotives that still stands.

DIESEL POWER

The last steam powered locomotives produced in Britain came into service in the late 1940s. A new and more efficient power source was being developed.

The diesel-electric locomotive uses a diesel engine to drive a generator which in turn powers electric motors connected to the driving wheels. Diesel-electric locomotives have proved themselves clean and very reliable. They have provided the motive power for a large number of trains since the 1950s.

The *HST 125* (High Speed Train) is an example of a modern high speed diesel-electric passenger train. It uses two streamlined power cars at the front and rear of the train to reach an operational speed of 201 km/h (125 mph—hence the name). Each power unit has a lightweight V-12 diesel engine rated at 1678.5 kw (2250 hp) and each provides the power for four electric motors. The trains are designed for reliable operation on existing track. A prototype *HST 125* reached 230 km/h (143 mph) in tests. The train entered regular service in 1976. The coaches are air conditioned and air suspended.

An improved version of the *HST 125*, the *XPT*, is now going into service in Australia.

ELECTRIC POWER

Diesel-electric locomotives carry their own fuel (oil) with them. Oil

Above: The HST 125 which is in regular use providing a fast and comfortable passenger service on most routes in the British Isles. Like most modern high speed trains the HST 125 uses power units that are an integral part of the train.

is not now the cheapest way of generating electric power and also larger generators are more efficient. It makes sense to generate electrical power centrally and distribute this power directly to the train motors—via overhead cables or additional rails. The initial high cost of the distribution system can be recovered from much lower operational costs. Many countries now use electric power for their railway systems. In Britain part of the system is electrified and it was decided to use an electric locomotive for the next generation of high speed trains—the *APT*.

APT

There is a limit to the speed at which trains can travel on normal railway lines. The angle of camber (tilt) on the corners sets the maximum speed of the train—as at higher speeds a train might leave the rails. Two solutions are possible to this problem—build new railway lines designed only for higher speed trains or allow the train to tilt itself.

The revolutionary Advanced Passenger Train is designed to tilt as much as 9° while the train negotiates corners. The tilting mechanism is extremely complex and requires computer control.

Designed to travel on existing tracks at speeds exceeding 240 km/h (150 mph), the *APT* collects overhead electric power at 25,000 volts and steps this down to run four 746 kw (1000 hp) motors which are mounted in the power cars at the centre of the train.

Basic work began on the *APT* in the 1960s but there have been major problems with the tilting mechanism and the *APT* is not yet in passenger service.

Other countries have approached the problem of high speed trains by building new tracks. In Japan the *Shinkansen* (which is also known as the *Bullet* train because of the shape of its rounded nose) is capable of travelling at speeds of up to 257 km/h (160 mph) on a special line. This line is a wider guage than standard lines in Japan and is constructed to be as straight and level as possible. Spectacular bridges and viaducts help to make the *Skinkansen* rail routes some of the most impressive in the world. 25,000 volt overhead power is stepped down to drive 64 185 kw (248 hp) motors in the 16 car trains. Every axle on the train has a motor and this enables the train to accelerate extremely rapidly. The first *Shinkansen* line came into service in 1964 and now much of Japan is served by these trains providing rapid and efficient communication.

The *Shinkansen* uses an in-cab signalling system. Information on track conditions are sent directly to the cab. If an earthquake occurs (these are frequent in Japan) all trains stop automatically. The speed of the train is also controlled from a central control point—increasing the safety of the system.

TGV

The French solution to the problem of developing high speed trains was, like with the Japanese *Shinkansen* train, to lay down new and much more highly engineered tracks with steeply cambered corners. These tracks were to be in addition to their existing ones. This decision was aided by the fact that the French railways were already being used to their capacity.

Work began on the development of the train and tracks in 1968. Initially the power unit was to be gas-turbine but, after a first prototype was built, electric propulsion was chosen.

The first electric prototype achieved a speed of 260 km/h (161 mph) within one month of test running.

The *TGV* (Train à Grande Vitesse —which means high speed train) went into service in 1981. It has pantograph pickups for both 25,000 volts AC or 1500 volts DC for use in different areas of the rail system. A number of trains also have a third pantograph for operation on the 15,000 volt Swiss system.

Each of the train's two power cars have six 524 kw (704 hp) motors which drive the eight wheels on the power unit and the four wheels on the first bogie of the next carriage. Each driven bogie has a separate power unit to reduce problems caused by loss of power—should a unit fail.

The weight of the train has been carefully considered and minimized. Computer models and wind tunnel tests have reduced the aerodynamic drag. These factors combine to enable the train to negotiate gradients of up to 1 in 30 with little loss of speed.

Right: *TGV* **and track was designed for high speed.**

The track is carefully laid on extra firm foundations to eliminate subsidence problems. The minimum radius for a curve in the track is 4 km (2.5 miles) and the angle of the curves are optimized for a *TGV* at maximum speed.

WORLD SPEED RECORD

In 1981 a *TGV* equipped with larger wheels and modified gearing, primarily to test the track at high speed, set a world speed record of 437 km/h (236 mph). Regular trains travel at about 265 km/h (165 mph) but these speeds are expected to increase.

The *TGV* has a sophisticated in-cab control and display system based on the system developed for the Japanese *Shinkansen* train. Information is passed to and from the train by track signals controlling speed, braking and warnings. The driver of the train receives information as to the speed he should be travelling at, and once he has set that speed, the computers on board will maintain the speed.

Standard trackside signals are not used. The track is divided into 2.1 km (1.3 miles) sections which give information back to a central control station on the positions of each train on the tracks. No two trains are allowed to occupy the same section of track. Trains are normally slowed to a halt over four track sections.

There are three braking circuits which operate in succession or

Fact file . . .

The TGV saves an hour on the journey time of conventional trains on the Paris—Dijon route and over two hours on the Paris—Geneva route. With a high standard of passenger comfort and stations in the heart of cities the TGV is a strong rival to air travel.

TGV—High Speed Train

Right: The top two illustrations show computer drawings of the front of the train which were used in the development of the aerodynamics.

The bottom photograph shows a model undergoing wind tunnel tests.

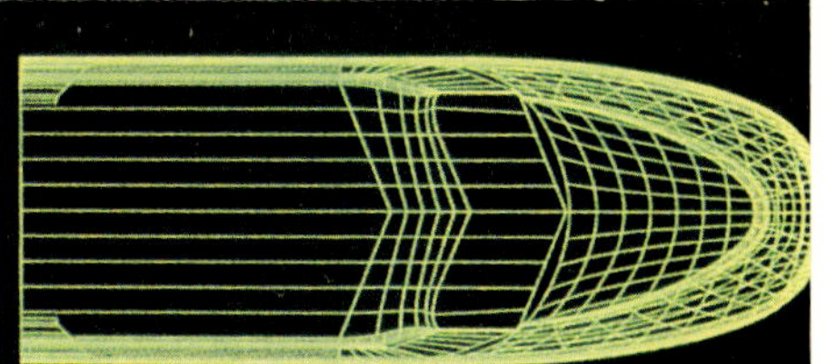

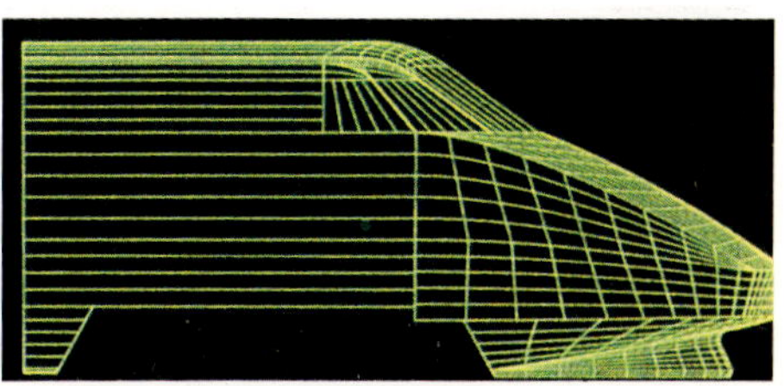

together. The first operates by turning the motors into generators (the energy produced being lost as heat), the second by the use of disc brakes and the third by brake pads on the wheel tracks. In an emergency the train can stop in 3.1 km (1.86 miles).

The trains consist of ten coach sets. The intermediate coaches are articulated (they share a common bogie), and springing and suspension are designed to give a smooth ride at speed.

The *TGV* system was originally criticized as being very expensive to develop and build but the system has proved itself to be more successful than more complicated tilting systems such as the *APT*.

FUTURE TRAINS

Below: An artist's impression of a proposed pneumatic suspended rail system. Pistons in the sealed tube above the vehicle would be propelled along by differences in air pressure created by remote pumping stations.

The supertrains of today—the *Shinkansen, TGV* and *APT*, have one thing in common with all other trains—they ride on metal flanged driving wheels on metal tracks. There is a limit to the speed and efficiency of such a system. It is likely that future train systems operating at higher speeds will depend on new means of propulsion and support.

Raised tracks using single rail (monorail) support are a popular idea for carrying the train of tomorrow. In this case the train would be suspended below a raised track supported by either metal or concrete pillars.

PNEUMATIC RAILWAY

The pneumatic or atmospheric railway was first demonstrated in the 19th century. A close fitting piston in a cast iron pipe was attached to the bottom of a railway carriage. At intervals along the line steam engines would pump air out of the cast iron pipe. The piston, and hence the railway train attached to it, would be pushed along the pipe by the difference in atmospheric pressure in front of and behind the piston. An experimental system did operate but problems with the airtight seals (rats ate them!) made the system impractical at the time.

Now a new version of the pneumatic railway using modern materials is being developed. Designed for urban use, the pneumatic system would be extremely quiet and non polluting.

THE LINEAR MOTOR

One of the most interesting developments for use in the next generation of high speed trains is the linear induction motor. Unlike the normal type of electric motor, which provides rotary power to drive gears and wheels, the linear motor produces power in a straight line. If an aluminium (stator) rail is placed between the poles of the motor, a railway vehicle carrying the motor will be propelled directly along the track. Losses due to slipping and gearing are eliminated and a train using this system can reach very high speeds.

MAGNETIC LEVITATION

A train using linear motors for propulsion can still travel on wheels for support but at very high speeds this would need absolutely straight tracks with no imperfections.

One solution to this problem

would be to support the train on a cushion of air like a hovercraft. Several experimental systems using this method have been tried but there are difficulties in regulating and guiding the vehicle to give a smooth ride.

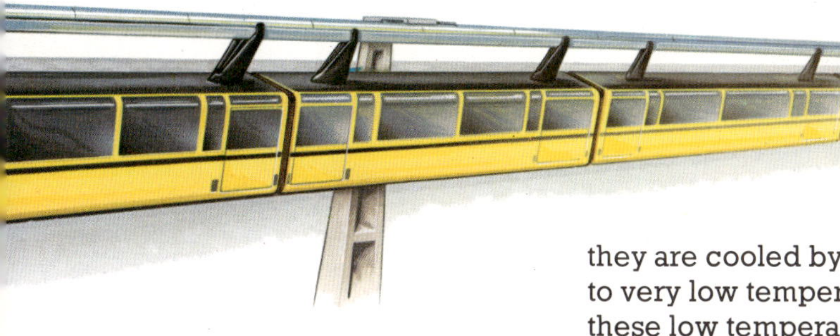

Now, however, a better solution is available in the form of magnetic levitation which is quiet and has no moving parts.

Magnetic levitation was developed from the linear motor. Electromagnetic coils on the bottom of the railway vehicle are used to generate powerful magnetic fields. If this field is placed over another field of similar polarity (this time produced by permanent magnets on the track) the two fields repel each other and the railway vehicle will float above

the track. There is little friction and the vehicle can accelerate to very high speeds easily. Adjusting the shape of the fields can guide the vehicle around curves in the track.

To increase the strength of the field produced by the lifting coils they are cooled by liquid helium to very low temperatures. At these low temperatures the coils of the electromagnets become superconducting and produce an intense magnetic field with very low power usage.

Many variations on this type of suspension system have been tried experimentally in various countries.

Japanese National Railways have been running an experimental high speed maglev vehicle on a test track. The test vehicle had reached speeds of 207 km/h (192 mph) by 1980. Electromagnets were placed on the test track instead of on the vehicle.

Designs for a maglev service to run between Tokyo's Narita Airport 65 km (40 miles) to the city centre in 40 minutes are being developed using the more economical approach of placing the electromagnets in the vehicle.

In Germany, a maglev vehicle some 54 metres (178 ft) in length called *Transrapid-06* has undergone tests on a track some 32 kilometres (20 miles) long. In this vehicle the levitation magnets are placed underneath the T-shaped track, lifting the vehicle by attraction instead of repulsion. Speeds in excess of 320 km/h (200 mph) have been achieved in test runs. Some 64 electromagnets provide levitation and an additional 56 electromagnets are used to guide the vehicle. When in service the *Transrapid-06* will carry 200 passengers in two cars at speeds of up to 400 km/h (250 mph).

Below: This is *Electra*, a model of British Rail's proposed design for the inter-city trains of the future. Intended for use on the London–Edinburgh East Coast Main Line, *Electra* should be in service by 1991.

RAILS AND CABLES

Railways are not only for the rapid and easy transport of people over great distances. Some rail systems are merely for local transportation within cities. Some use totally non standard means of support such as cables to cross difficult terrain. Some railways even have no destination at all—they are purely for pleasure.

THE ROLLER COASTER

A central part of most amusement parks is the roller coaster. A train of open carriages is sent around a track of steep inclines, twists and vertical loops in order to give the passengers an exciting and even terrifying ride.

Although the rides are constructed to give the impression of being dangerous they are actually constructed to very high safety standards. Often they use advanced technology to give ever more impressive rides.

Traditionally roller coasters are constructed of wood and concrete with heavy metal cars making up the trains.

New roller coasters are now being built with modern materials and design. They are faster, safer and more exciting than the earlier rides. The new designs are made from strong steel tubes. They can be shaped into many different curves and loops, and are strong enough to be almost self supporting.

The cars are made from light materials such as fibreglass and have built-in safety bars. There are two upper wheels and one lower wheel at each corner of the car. The upper wheels ride in the tubular track, whilst the lower wheels grip the rails underneath to reduce vibration and ensure a safe ride.

The power for the ride can be supplied by a giant electrical catapult or by a more complicated compressed air system. The trains of cars accelerate rapidly from the starting point.

A computer monitors and controls the whole complicated structure, which may include many miles of electrical circuits.

Roller coaster rides compete against each other to be ever more daring and thrilling. Corkscrews of looped turns and near vertical sections subject the passengers to strong gravitational forces. In some rides the cars pass through water troughs sending great plumes of spray out towards bystanders. Other rides switch the direction of the car's travel to disorientate the passengers.

Most modern roller coaster rides are made up of standard sections and the rides can be dismantled

Above left: The modern roller coaster is a lightweight construction of strong steel tubes laid out in a series of loops and curves to give an exciting ride.

Above: This early example of a cable car is seen crossing a fast flowing river. It is supported by six main cables and pulled along by another.

and reconstructed in a different form quite easily—the only limitation is the imagination of the designer.

THE CABLE CAR

In cable railways there are no locomotives—the cables from which the cars are suspended are drawn along by fixed engines at either end of the railway system. The cables are usually run in a continuous loop so that cars travelling in one direction then travel round the terminus and continue in the opposite direction parallel to their original course. This is particularly efficient when the cable system runs up a steep slope as the weight of cars coming up the slope is cancelled out by the weight of cars going down.

The most common form of cable car is the aerial car which is often seen on mountain slopes. The cables are supported by strong pylons at regular intervals. Often higher up the mountain the enclosed cars are replaced by lighter cable systems which carry individual skiers to the top of the more popular ski slopes.

Another form of mountain cable car is the Funicular railway which uses two cars running on parallel tracks to provide a similar service. In this case the cars change direction at each terminus. Some Funicular systems use water tanks on the downwards moving car to provide motive power.

The famous cable car system which runs up and down the steep main streets of San Francisco in the USA uses underground cables to power the cars. The cables are accessible through slots in the road. The cable cars clamp onto the underground cable, which is constantly in motion, whenever they wish to start moving.

TRAMCARS

Tramcars or Streetcars are railed vehicles which use overhead electric power in city streets. Originally designed to replace horse drawn public transport, the tramcar was thought until recently to have outlived its usefulness. The tramcar can cause congestion on modern urban roads because it is tied to the rails on which it travels.

However, the efficiency of its driving system, the lack of pollution and the ability to carry large numbers of passengers efficiently has led to renewed interest in this form of transport. Articulated trains or tramcars are carrying larger than ever number of passengers and new tram-only routes are being developed in cities.

Tramcars collect their power from overhead electric cables via long pantograph arms or poles. They can usually travel in either direction without turning around. Often the seating is reversible so that passengers can always face the direction of travel.

Many of the tramcars built in England were double decked to enable more passengers to be carried. The city of Sheffield which ran its last tramcar service more than 25 years ago is now planning to reintroduce a tramcar service.

Below: This tramcar in Zurich, Switzerland consists of two articulated units joined together to form a train. In much of Europe tramcars still play an important part in urban transport systems.

CHAPTER 3

SEA MACHINES

Using the depths of the oceans or their wind-blown surfaces, Man has designed and built vessels to transport himself, his cargoes and weapons all over the world. Giant supertankers plough through the waves, fast hydrofoil boats skim the surface, light hovercraft race across the sea and up onto the land, strong icebreakers crush their way through the polar ice sheets, passenger ferries ply the popular busy routes and, in case anyone gets into trouble, sturdy reliable lifeboats are there to rescue people from the angry sea. Today's ship designers are writing a new chapter in maritime history with novel, stronger and faster craft being developed.

The *Queen Elizabeth II (QE2)* is one of the world's most luxurious and well-designed ocean liners. Built in 1966 at Clydebank, Scotland, it is made of welded steel and weighs 67,140 gross tonnes, with a length of 293 m (963 ft) and a beam of 32 m (105 ft). It can cruise at a speed of 28.5 knots on its two steam turbine engines, providing 110,000 hp for its two giant propellers, weighing 32 tonnes apiece.

LIFEBOATS

If ever reliable craft were needed, it is the case with lifeboats. They must be sturdy, stable and buoyant. They must be fast, to get to the scene in time; supertough, to withstand the appalling conditions of gale-force winds and high seas; unsinkable and capable of righting themselves quickly if capsized. They must also be manoeuvrable, to get close to the distressed ship. Although there is no substitute for the bravery and courage of the crew, the design of the lifeboat and its equipment is of paramount importance to the safety and effectiveness of marine rescue.

The latest in lifeboat design is the 15.8 m (52 ft)-long *Arun* class. It is constructed of GRP (glass reinforced plastic or glass fibre). Sealed watertight compartments are built throughout its length. The hull is made of a double skin, with expanded polyurethane foam in between the outer and inner skins, to keep the boat afloat if all the compartments are flooded. The wheelhouse and other structures on deck are made of tough welded aluminium. Two 280 kw (375 hp) marine diesel engines power the boat, giving it a top speed of 18 knots.

The wheelhouse itself, the 'brain' of the lifeboat, is equipped with the latest in navigational aids— automatic pilot, echo-sounders, radar and radio-direction finders. Communications with shore, sea and air services are vital during a rescue and VHF and MF radio equipment is used. The wheelhouse can be made waterproof by an airlock door system, to protect this valuable equipment should the boat capsize.

The array of specialized rescue equipment on board is impressive. Each lifeboat carries two emergency life-rafts and two inflatable dinghies. The breeches buoy is a vital piece of gear. It consists of a harness or small seat suspended on a thick rope, which is fired by rocket gun from the lifeboat to the stricken vessel. This forms a lifeline and, one by one, people are hauled along the rope to safety. Another piece of important gear is the drogue, a cone-shaped bag of canvas or wire mesh which is towed behind the lifeboat. This creates a drag and steadies the boat in high seas.

There is access from the wheelhouse below decks, to the crew's quarters and engine room. Thus there is no need for anyone to go on deck in stormy weather until necessary. Then floodlights on deck and a loudhailer system help the crew in their work. A parachute flare set off at night lights up the whole area around the boat. Besides all the medical supplies and stretchers, there are lifelines, protective clothing, extra life-jackets, fire-fighting and oxygen equipment, all tucked away under watertight hatches around the boat.

LIFEBOAT TRIALS

A modern lifeboat is a very special craft. Scale models of the design are subjected to rigorous testing for months in experimental wave tanks under the most extreme conditions. On average, 2–3 m (6–10 ft) waves are simulated in the tank, with occasional 'giant' waves. Sections of the hull are put under enormous hydraulic pressure, far in excess of anything likely to be experienced at sea, to test their strength.

Finally, the lifeboat itself is put to sea for further tests, such as the 'parbuckling' trial. This is a self-righting test and every lifeboat must pass to be declared seaworthy. The parbuckle is a long thick rope suspended from a crane and attached to the lifeboat. As the crane lifts, the boat is deliberately capsized, the rope released and the boat left to right itself. If all goes well, it should be floating right way up in five to eight seconds. This is achieved by a system of water tanks controlled by special valves and is explained fully in the diagram below.

For years designers have looked for ways of increasing the speed of a lifeboat without sacrificing its stability. The secret lies in the form of the hull. In the early 1960s, the US Coastguard Service designed a 13.4 m (44 ft) long, steel-hulled boat, powered with twin 200 hp (150 kw) engines and capable of 14 knots. This became known as the *Waveney* class and a few are still in service in British waters today. In 1973, the *Thames* class of lifeboat was designed, with a length of 15.2 m (50 ft) and a speed of 17.5 knots when powered with a 425 hp (318 kw) diesel engine. Then, in the late 1970s, the *Arun* class

Right: Speed is of the essence in inshore rescue work. The 'rubber duck', high-speed inflatable dinghy is capable of 29 knots with twin 50 hp (37 kw) engines and is invaluable for work in shallow waters.

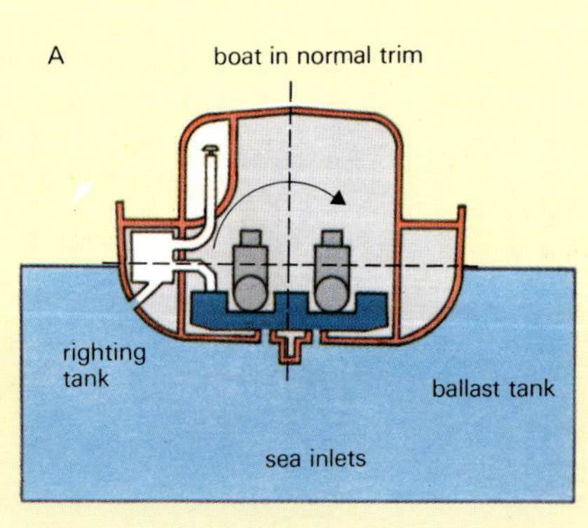

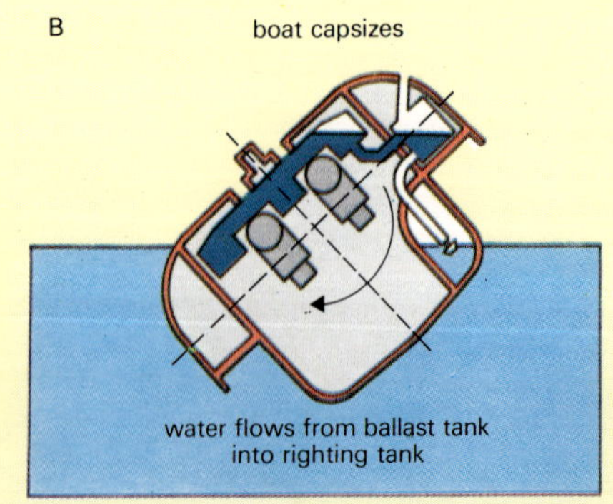

superseded the *Thames*, with a top speed of 18 knots.

For inshore rescue, 'rubber ducks' are used. These are high-speed inflatable dinghies of the *Atlantic* class. The latest design is 6 m (21 ft) long, made of neoprene-proofed nylon and capable of 29 knots using two 50 hp (37 kw) engines. The Royal National Lifeboat Institute (RNLI) of Britain has 120 of these fast craft in service today.

Lifeboat design and marine rescue knows no political boundaries and international cooperation is seen here at its best. The lifeboat service has come a long way from the days when men would row out in a wooden boat to rescue people at sea. The French were the first to test a rescue boat with buoyancy tanks in 1765. The British followed, in 1785, with a similar model. A lifeboat buoyed up with hydrogen tanks was tested by the USA in 1816.

Above: The modern *Arun* class lifeboat will stay afloat and upright even if all its 26 watertight compartments are holed.

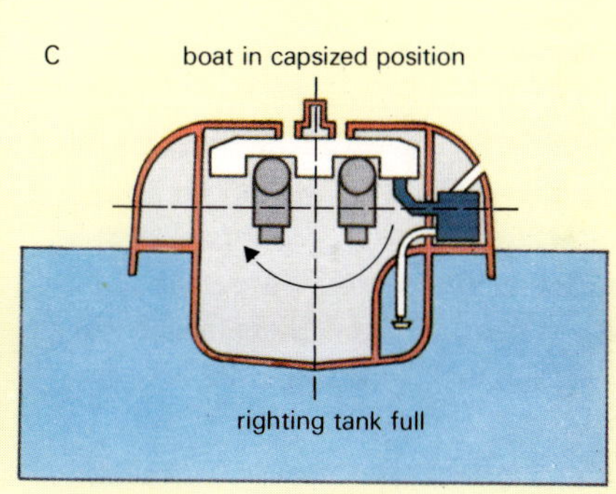

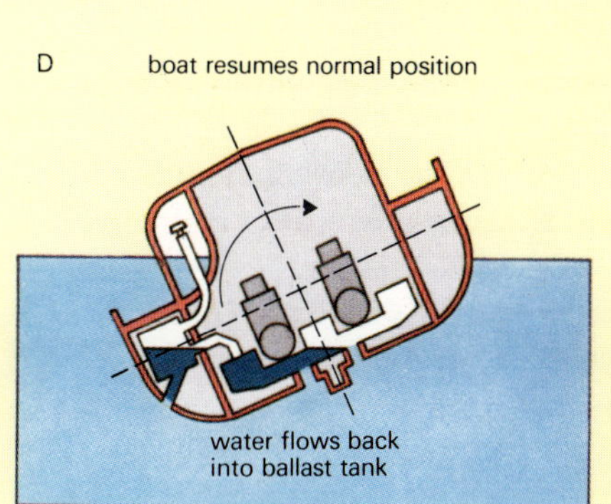

The Oakley self-righting system was named after its inventor Richard Oakley, a marine architect. As the boat capsizes, water in the ballast tank flows into the righting tank on the port (left) side. The weight of water turns the boat through 180°, back to the upright position. This five to eight second operation is ingeniously controlled by a system of specially designed valves.

ICE-BREAKERS

There is nothing subtle about icebreakers. They are big, heavy ships designed to do just that—break through the ice that presents one of the most formidable and dangerous barriers to shipping in polar seas. The disaster of the *Titanic* in 1912 shows the destructive force of ice. It can puncture the steel-plated hull of a ship with ease.

A weight of 61,000 tonnes is sure to break most thicknesses of ice. The world's most powerful, purpose-built icebreaker was built in 1982, designed to work along the USSR's Arctic coastline. The USSR also launched the longest icebreaker in 1983, the *Rossiya*, with a length of 140 m (460 ft) and a weight of 25,000 tonnes. Both ships are nuclear-powered. But 24 years even before this, in 1959, the USSR had built the world's first nuclear-powered ice-breaker, the *Lenin*.

The USSR is among several nations that must, of necessity, have powerful and efficient icebreakers since its northern seaports along the Arctic coast are ice-bound for much of the year. Without the services of ice-breakers, the shipping lanes would remain closed. The situation is the same for the northern ports of Canada, Alaska and the Great Lakes area of the USA.

Ships can also be converted into icebreakers. The SS *Manhattan*, a huge American oil tanker, almost 300 m (1000 ft) long, was converted to an icebreaker by the addition of an armoured prow, 21 m (69 ft) long, and massive internal framing for strength. Its engine has a high power of 43,000 shp (shaft horsepower) on twin shafts. The *Manhattan* successfully navigated a North-West Passage, from Newfoundland to Alaska's Prudhoe Bay, in 1969 opening a new route to the Arctic oil fields.

A well-designed icebreaker can force its way through ice up to 10.7 m (35 ft) thick. It has a special hull design and a wide beam, with a relatively flat bottom. A recent development in the Finnish *Ermak* polar icebreaker is the double-hull construction of the ship and the watertight compartments throughout its length. An icebreaker's bow is spoon-shaped and set at an angle, usually 30° to the horizontal. The wide beam prevents chunks of ice damaging the propeller blades and also cuts a broad path so that narrower hulled ships can follow safely in its wake. The propellers are sited deep beneath the hull, sometimes surrounded by a metal duct for further protection, and they are made of cast steel.

The method of ice breaking is rather crude, with the ship running at speed up and over the edge of the ice. The sheer weight of the vessel crushes and cracks the ice. Ramming at full speed is a last resort in very thick ice.

The Norwegian company *Aker* have designed a semi-submersible ice-breaking tanker (SSIT) which

Above: A nuclear-powered icebreaker of the *Lenin* class, named after the first ship of this type built by the USSR in 1959. The power is produced by two water-cooled nuclear reactors which can develop 75,000 shp for almost indefinite periods. This is an invaluable feature since many months have to be spent at sea by such ships clearing the ice-bound northern seaports to keep shipping lanes open.

Top: Stuck fast in polar ice, this icebreaker is useless. If the ship is fitted with an air-bubbling system, it can get free. This involves streams of pressurized air being squeezed out of small holes below the waterline. On rising to the surface, the bubbles act as a lubricant to the hull and loosen the ice around the ship. Without this system, another icebreaker may have to tow the stricken vessel out.

could, at least in theory, go under the ice and then pump out its water ballast, causing it to rise. With its permanent ballast of cement or liquid mud giving the SSIT a weight of 40,000 tonnes, the uplifting force of the vessel cracks the ice.

A wonderfully simple way of breaking ice was discovered in the early 1980s, almost by accident. By running a hovercraft over the ice at a speed of 20–30 knots, the ice breaks quite quickly. Pressure waves are set up within the ice and radiate out from the hovercraft along lines of weakness. Slowing down the hovercraft has the same result. Here, the downward air pressure of the slow-moving craft pushes down the water below the ice sheet, forming an air cavity. This moves along with the hovercraft and the ice eventually begins to sag under its own weight since it has no support from the water below. Hovercraft are particularly economic as they use little energy. They are also wide and clear a broad path astern. And they can

operate in shallow waters. The thickness of the ice, however, limits their effectiveness, although ice a metre or more thick can be continuously broken at speeds of 12–30 knots. The National Research Council of Canada is developing a prototype of an air-cushion vehicle attached to a conventional ship and this is proving most successful.

If a ship is unfortunate enough to get stuck fast in ice, a recent development by the Finnish company *Wartsila* will help. The system can be fitted to existing ships and consists of feeding air under pressure along pipes that run within the ship's hull. The air is squeezed out through a line of small holes well below the waterline and rises to the surface as a sheet of bubbles along the length of the submerged hull. This has the effect of 'lubricating' the hull and loosening up the ice around it. Once the ship is free, streams of bubbles can be blown out at intervals to prevent the ice closing in again.

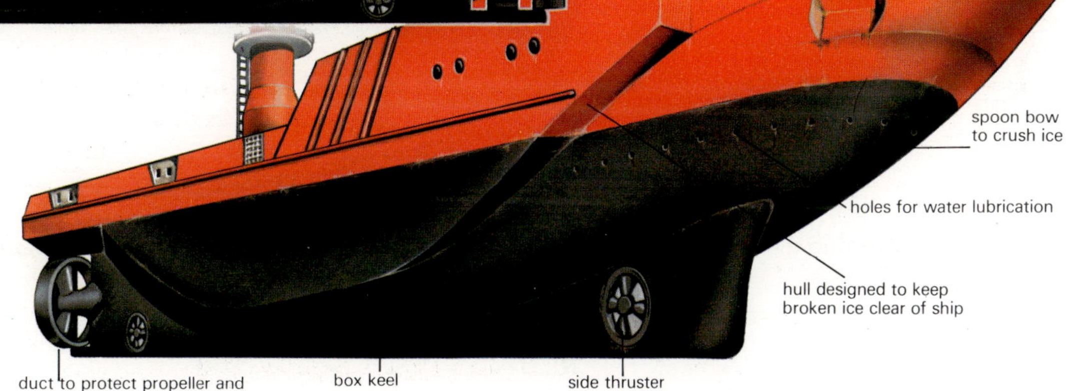

The *Canmar Kigoriak* Icebreaker, Anchor Handling Tug and Supply Ship

Right: The *Canmar Kigoriak* shows the typical design features of a modern ice-breaker. Note the spoon-shaped bow with sharp ice-crushing angle; propeller set deep in the hull; holes below waterline for escape of air bubbles; the hull's shape designed to keep broken ice away.

STENA CONSTRUCTOR

A new breed of all-weather, multi-purpose ships has been built with the advent of offshore oil drilling. Called 'support ships', they service oil rigs all over the world.

They deliver supplies, men and machines to the oil rig. They act as back-up vessels for underwater diving operations and house the divers in pressurized conditions during their weeks of work. They can deal with emergency situations, such as a fire or a blowout on the rig. They can serve as a lifeboat, to rescue the crew in severe storms or airlift accident victims to safety.

Such a ship is the *Stena Constructor*. Built by the Swedish Stena line and tested in 1979, it is an immense stable vessel, with accommodation for 300 people. Weighing some 4000 tonnes, its overall length is 111 m (366 ft), with a beam of 20.5 m (67 ft)—a length-to-breadth ratio of about five to one.

The afterdeck of the *Stena Constructor* is long and flat. Here, cargo is stored and transferred to the oil rig by crane. In rough seas, this is a tricky business. The position of the ship must be maintained (called 'station keeping') by powerful thrusts of the main and side propellers. The main propeller and side-thrusters are electrically driven by huge generators and powered through electric motors, each side-thruster receiving 1120 kw (1500 hp) apiece. The main propeller is driven by no less than four 1500 hp motors. Each propeller has a controllable blade pitch so that the thrust can be varied and even reversed. Such a powerful system can hold the ship in position, without drift, in a Force 9 gale (41–47 knots), with 7 m (23 ft) waves and a cross current of 4 knots.

The superstructure of the ship contains the wheelhouse and control rooms with sophisticated electronic equipment for navigation and diving operations. Immediately aft of the superstructure is the diving area, consisting of five vertical levels and geared for 12 divers. There is a three-man diving bell, about 1.9 m (6 ft) in diameter, which is lowered through a hatch in the ship's bottom called a monopool. Divers can work at depths of 450 m (1500 ft) in this pressurized sphere. Since some tasks may take several weeks to complete, the divers live in decompression chambers on board, not returning to normal atmospheric pressure until the job is done.

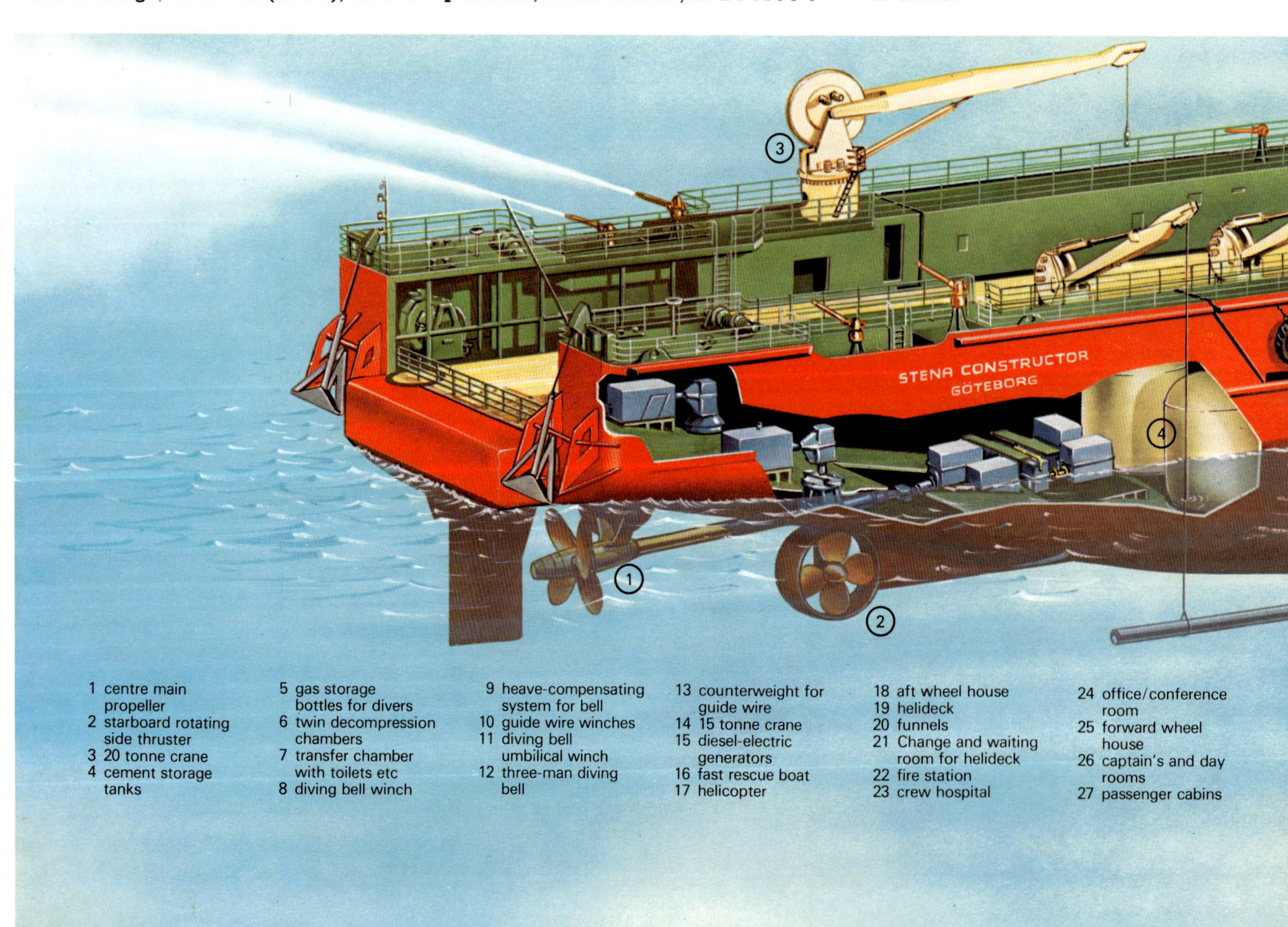

1	centre main propeller	
2	starboard rotating side thruster	
3	20 tonne crane	
4	cement storage tanks	
5	gas storage bottles for divers	
6	twin decompression chambers	
7	transfer chamber with toilets etc	
8	diving bell winch	
9	heave-compensating system for bell	
10	guide wire winches	
11	diving bell umbilical winch	
12	three-man diving bell	
13	counterweight for guide wire	
14	15 tonne crane	
15	diesel-electric generators	
16	fast rescue boat	
17	helicopter	
18	aft wheel house	
19	helideck	
20	funnels	
21	Change and waiting room for helideck	
22	fire station	
23	crew hospital	
24	office/conference room	
25	forward wheel house	
26	captain's and day rooms	
27	passenger cabins	

The Swedish *Stena Constructor*, built in 1979 to repair and maintain oil rigs, support divers, and act as a rescue and fire-fighting vessel—an all-purpose saviour, weighing 4000 tonnes with a length of 111 m (366 ft) and a beam of 20.5 m (67 ft). The distinctive helicopter pad (below) above the bridge takes a Sikorsky 61N which can carry 25 passengers.

28 rescue rooms
29 kongsberg surface reference radar
30 kongsberg computer positioning room
31 bow thrusters in transverse tunnels

THE FERRY

Car ferries are an increasingly popular way for people to travel on holiday. Today's ferries are as large, and often as comfortable, as the ocean-going liners of grander days. The largest car ferry is called the GTS *Finnjet* and it travels across the Baltic Sea from Helsinki in Finland to Travemünde in West Germany. Built in 1977, it can carry 350 cars and over 1500 passengers, and attain a speed of 30.5 knots.

The design of ferries poses problems for the marine architect because of the limited space available which must accommodate so many uses, such as passengers and crew, cabins, cars, heavy commercial vehicles, and eating, drinking and recreational facilities. The designer cannot simply pile on more decks since the ship will become unstable and yet the deck area must be spacious and uncluttered, for vehicles and people alike. At the same time, the trip must not take too long or be too expensive, so the ship must be built for speed and economy. Because of the seasonal nature of holidays, the engines and other machinery have to be powerful enough to meet tight summer schedules and yet economic to run on the slower off-peak journeys. All in all, the designer of a car ferry has to compromise to fulfil all these conflicting needs.

Ferries are typically arranged on several levels. Vehicles are driven on at the after end and parked on the lowest levels, immediately above the water line. Passenger amenities and accommodation are on three or four levels above this. The cabins are usually placed at the forward end, and bars, discos and cinemas at the after end where noise and vibration are higher.

When the last vehicle is on board, the ramps are pulled up, like a drawbridge, and closed securely to form a watertight seal. Since the front of the ship takes a heavier battering from the waves, the bow is made of tough shell plating which hinges together under hydraulic power. An inner door backs up the bow plates and is operated by hydraulic jigger winches. The whole front section lifts up, like a visor, when the ship is berthed, to allow the cars off. The vehicle decks can be changed and rearranged to cater for different types of vehicle. If a lot of commercial trucks, coaches and caravans are expected, plenty of headroom is needed and so the decks can be heightened. In peak holiday time, additional car decks can be put in and then stowed away against bulk heads when not in use.

Vehicle decks must be well-ventilated to carry away poisonous exhaust fumes. When engines are switched on prior to off-loading, a system of fans effects a complete change of air on deck every few minutes. Fire sensors continuously monitor the decks and if fire does

break out, automatic extinguishers douse the flames with water, gas or powder. At the touch of a button, fireproof doors seal off the passenger areas.

Ferries travel along the busiest shipping routes in the world. Seamanship and navigational skills are vital, as is the latest in electronic gear. Two multi-range radars give a continuous plot of the movements of other ships and a warning is sounded if the ferry's course will bring it too close to another's path.

Left and below left: The ferry *Olau Hollandia* has all the comfort and speed needed for cross-channel travel. It is over 150 m (495 ft) long, 25 m (83 ft) wide and weighs 13,500 tonnes. There are three large car decks, many cabins, and recreational areas including a full-size swimming pool, sauna, gymnasium and solarium.

Right: Once berthed, the hinged shell plates of the bow open for offloading.

AIRCRAFT CARRIERS

The largest of the large warships, aircraft carriers are giant, floating military bases. During World War II, they were the fleet's most powerful weapon. They were protected by smaller battleships that would take on the enemy if they got too close.

The problem these days is the great cost of building such craft: the US *Nimitz* class of carrier, the largest in the world, cost about $3 billion (£2½ million) each. And there is also the problem that if a carrier is hit by a submarine's torpedo or an airborne missile, all its planes sink with it. The traditional carrier is now considered a 'sitting duck' target and it may not be the best design for the future. Other options are being considered, such as building many smaller carriers with shorter flight decks which would accommodate armed helicopters and vertical and short take-off and landing (V/STOL) planes. Looking at the design of three carrier types —American, Soviet and British—will illustrate today's trends.

The American *Nimitz* carriers are the world's largest, with a displacement of 91,487 tonnes. They are 323 m (1092 ft) long and have almost 2 hectares (4½ acres) of deck space. Four nuclear-powered steam turbine engines drive the ship at a speed in excess of 30 knots (56 km/h or 35 mph). The radioactive core has a life of 13 years before it needs replacing. But if the carrier

Left: The nuclear-powered US *Nimitz* carriers reach speeds of over 30 knots. Two aircraft a minute can take-off from the angled flight deck. Below: Britain's trend-setting *Invincible* carrier has a 'ski jump' port-side and a smaller deck area for helicopters and jump jets.

The Invincible Class — HMS Illustrious

was at war, support ships would have to bring supplies such as fuel for the aircraft, ammunition and general stores every two weeks.

The USS *Enterprise* carrier is the longest warship ever built. It measures 336 m (1102 ft) in length. Its flight deck is set at an angle to the rest of the deck to give a clear path for planes landing and taking off. There is room for about 100 aircraft on deck and two can take to the air every minute. Each type of aircraft has a different function. There are fighter *Tomcat* jets, anti-submarine *Vikings* and *Sea King* helicopters. There are reconnaissance aircraft and planes with complex radar systems to give the carrier early warning of an enemy's approach. And, of course, there is the strike force, with planes like the *Intruder* and *Corsair* armed with tactical nuclear weapons. The carrier has only a few weapons to defend itself (some missiles and Gatling-type guns) and relies heavily on its own aircraft and escort of other fighting ships. A crew of 6000 people are needed to handle such a ship. Information from other ships, aircraft, satellite and shore is processed by computer.

The USSR's modern carriers are called *Kievs* and weigh about 32,000 tonnes. They are much smaller than the American carriers, but like them, they have an angled flight deck. They carry over 20 helicopters and 12 vertical take-off fighter planes. The forward third of the deck is armed with an array of weaponry, both to defend the carrier itself and to attack the enemy. Unlike the American vessels, these Soviet carriers can take part in an offensive. It is thought that the Soviets are currently building a new fleet of nuclear-powered carriers.

Britain's Royal Navy commissioned the *Ark Royal* carrier in 1984. It is small in comparison to the US carriers, being 206 m (677 ft) long. Four Rolls Royce gas turbine engines give it a speed of 28 knots. The *Invincible* class of carrier, launched in 1979, has a unique feature on the flight deck. On the port side, there is a ramp, called the 'ski jump', sloping upward at an angle of 7°. (Later designs will have a 15° slope.) *Sea Harrier* jump jets have a short take-off run up the ramp and are launched into the air. This means that they do not need to carry the extra fuel for a vertical take-off and, being lighter, they can stay airborne longer.

HMS Illustrious Dimensions	
Length, overall	209.6m
Length, waterline	192.8m
Breadth, flight deck	31.9m
Draught	6.5m
Standard displacement	16,000 tonnes
Performance	
Maximum speed	40km/h
	1847

NUCLEAR SUBMARINES

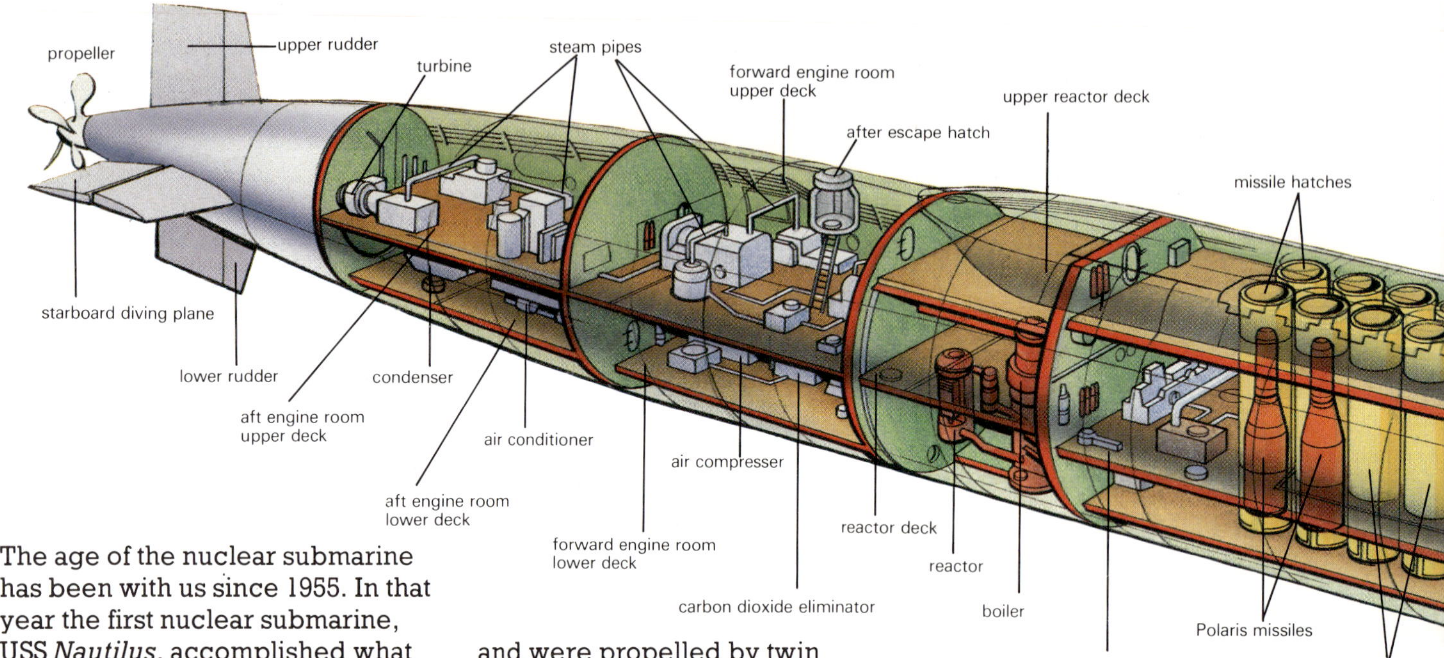

The age of the nuclear submarine has been with us since 1955. In that year the first nuclear submarine, USS *Nautilus*, accomplished what no other vessel had done before. It passed under the polar icecap from the Pacific side to the Atlantic side, surfacing near Iceland.

In the 30 years of development since then, nuclear submarines have become the most independent, most formidable and most dangerous vessels in the sea. They are independent because they can spend indefinite periods of time with no outside contact, since their nuclear reactor core only needs replacing every few years. The only limit to their time at sea is the endurance of the crew itself —how long can the men stand the isolated, cramped existence? They are formidable, because of the array of sophisticated computer-controlled equipment that runs them. And dangerous, because of the weapons they carry—ballistic missiles armed with dozens of nuclear warheads, with familiar names such as Polaris, Poseidon and Trident.

USS *Nautilus*, completed in 1954, was 97.2 m (319 ft) long and had a surface displacement of 3750 tonnes. From this model came the *Skate* class of American submarine, which were shorter (81.7 m/268 ft) and lighter (2550 tonnes). But they were not very efficient underwater. They were built for surface-running and were propelled by twin screws. New design of the hull made submarines more efficient and faster underwater. The shape was radically changed, to a round blunt front tapering to a sharply pointed after end, with a single propeller. The USS *Albacore* was one of the first with this design and it reached speeds in excess of 33 knots. The *Skipjack* class of high-speed submarines followed.

The USSR's modern *Alfa* class are the fastest submarines in the world, with a maximum speed of 42 knots (78 km/49 miles per hour). Such submarines can dive to 762 m (2500 ft).

Modern nuclear submarines are built for speed and for silent, easy running through the depths. The shape is very like that of a whale: streamlined like a torpedo, with hydroplanes where a whale would have fins—two on either side at the front and two at the 'tail' end. There is also a vertical rudder at the after end. To resist the enormous pressure of the water at depth, the submarine is made of steel plates welded together. It has a circular cross-section which is the strongest shape possible. The only structure interrupting its smooth outline is the tall conning tower, which contains the exhaust system, periscopes and radio masts and is the first part of

This cross-section of a *Polaris* nuclear submarine shows the torpedoes at the forward end and the *Polaris* intercontinental ballistic missiles in silos amidships. Each missile has a range of 4500 km (2800 miles), is armed with several nuclear warheads and can be launched from great depths. The design of the high-speed *Skipjack* submarines was adapted for *Polaris*. Each missile is about 10 m (33 ft) long and since they are stocked upright, *Polaris* submarines had a humpback.

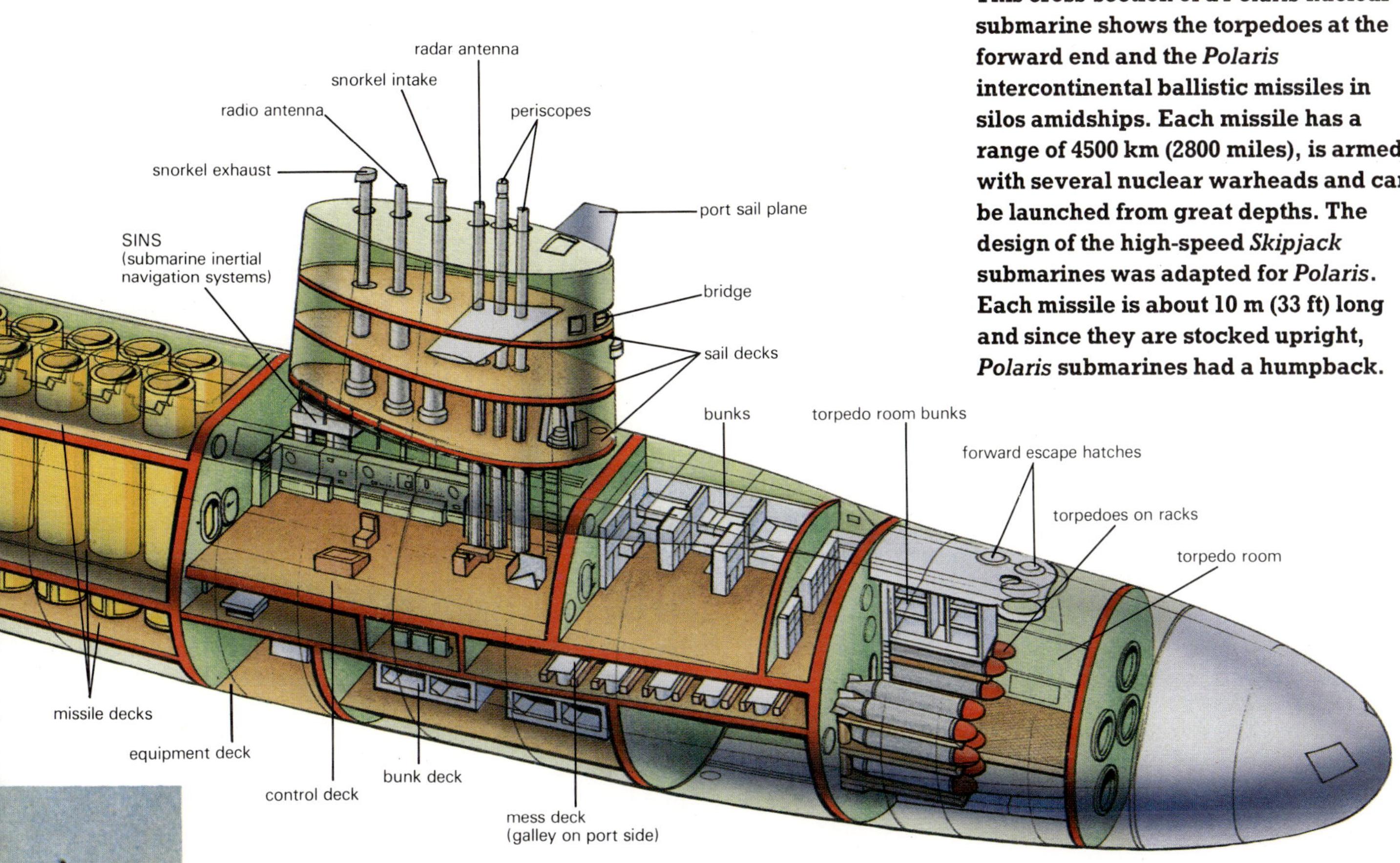

Left: USS *Whale*, one of the first American nuclear submarines, surfaced at the north pole in 1959. A nuclear submarine is powered by a nuclear reactor with a radioactive core. This is surrounded by a jacket through which water, under pressure, is pumped. The water is heated by the nuclear reaction in the core and then forced around a closed circuit of piping. It passes through a boiler or heat exchanger where it gives up most of its heat as steam. This passes through valves and powers the main propulsion turbines which drive the submarine. It also powers the turbo-generators and auxiliary turbines for other systems.

the submarine to break surface. All the openings in the hull (for example the access and escape hatches, missile silos and torpedo tubes) are equipped with watertight valves which are tested to full diving pressure.

When a submarine wants to dive, the ballast tanks are flooded with water and the powerful hydroplanes point its nose downward. It is driven underwater by the motor giving thrust to the single propeller and the aft hydroplanes steer its course. When it reaches the required depth, it levels off with the hydroplanes and some of the water is blown out of the main tanks with compressed air, until the craft is neutrally buoyant (neither too light nor too heavy). It simply hovers in midwater. To surface, compressed air is forced into the main tanks, filling them and expelling the remaining water. (This system was first used successfully in 1863 by the French submarine *Plongeur*.) The forward hydroplanes take the submarine up. The rudders and

hydroplanes are controlled by computer.

The most modern navigation aids are used in submarines today. Gone are the days when it was necessary to suface to take a reading by the stars. The submarine's position is continuously plotted by a 'dead-reckoning' system called a Ship Inertial Navigation System (SINS). This is capable of detecting acceleration rates in all three dimensions or planes, and computes the position automatically on charts. High-definition sonar and sideways-looking cameras tell of the surroundings and sensitive hydrophones pick up the least sound in the water. Radio communications are on very low frequency (VLF) wave bands, so that they will not be detected by the 'enemy', and the water absorbs the short wavelengths rapidly.

The United States and the Soviet Union are both believed to have installed ocean-bed and satellite-based submarine detection systems, but these are top secret.

HOVERCRAFT

A machine that glides above the surface of the sea at a speed of 70 knots, riding on a cushion of air over waves 3 m (10 ft) high—this is the hovercraft, invented in 1959 by a British engineer called Cockerell. Also known as an air-cushion vehicle (ACV) or a ground-effect vehicle (GEV), the principle behind the hovercraft is very simple. Air is forced down through the middle of the craft by large motor-driven fans. The flexible rubber skirt surrounding the bottom of the craft, traps this slightly compressed air underneath, so the whole vehicle is lifted up on a cushion of air, right off the surface. This method is so efficient that a craft of 100 tonnes can be lifted 0.3 m (1 ft) off the surface with very little pressure. (An ordinary car tyre needs 40–50 times more pressure.) Propellers or airscrews, like those of a plane, drive the hovercraft forward.

When hovercraft first came into commercial service, in the mid-1960s, the authorities could not decide whether they were ships or aeroplanes, or whether they were controlled by a captain or a pilot.

A hovercraft is a very versatile machine. Its advantage lies in being both a water and a land craft at the same time. It can cross the sea and run up a beach without stopping. It can travel overland on any flat surface, whether it be dirt tracks, roads, sand or swamps. It can skim over the frozen surface of lakes and rivers in the polar north, transporting vital cargo. It can even travel upstream against rapids because, since no part of it is underwater, it is not affected by the speed of the current. No special dock or landing strip is needed. The hovercraft simply does a 'belly flop' and sits down.

Since a hovercraft glides over the surface, there is hardly any friction created to slow it down. (Compare a ship which has to push itself through the waves, using energy all the time.) A hovercraft can therefore travel much faster than a ship and uses less power in doing so. Even carrying a full load of 416 people and 60 cars, the British Hovercraft Corporation's *SRN4 Mk III* cruises across the English Channel every day at speeds of 65–70 knots. The trip takes 30 minutes. The fastest hovercraft yet built is the American experimental *SES 100B*. It weighs 100 tonnes and can reach a speed of 90 knots.

Hovercraft have obvious advantages for military use. They can transport infantry and tanks to the centre of the fighting over surfaces that would halt other vehicles. The US Navy's Large Surface Effect Ship (LSES) looks like a small aircraft carrier. It was built by Bell Aerospace in 1981 and weighs 3000 tonnes. Vertical take-off planes can lift from its deck and it can travel faster than an ordinary carrier. Hovercraft can also pass over land and sea mines without setting them off. They can cross anti-submarine nets and low booms, and because they do not touch the water, they cannot be detected by radar. Torpedos can be fired from a hovercraft, but it cannot be hit itself —the torpedo simply goes underneath the hovering craft.

With all these advantages, surely the hovercraft is the 'air ship' of the future? Perhaps surprisingly, the answer is no. There are some real drawbacks to these craft. The first is economic. A hovercraft uses the same amount of power to lift itself no matter how slowly it is moving. Thus, it is only cheap to run when travelling at speed; at low speeds, a conventional ship is more economic. It cannot cope with waves higher than 3 m (10 ft). It

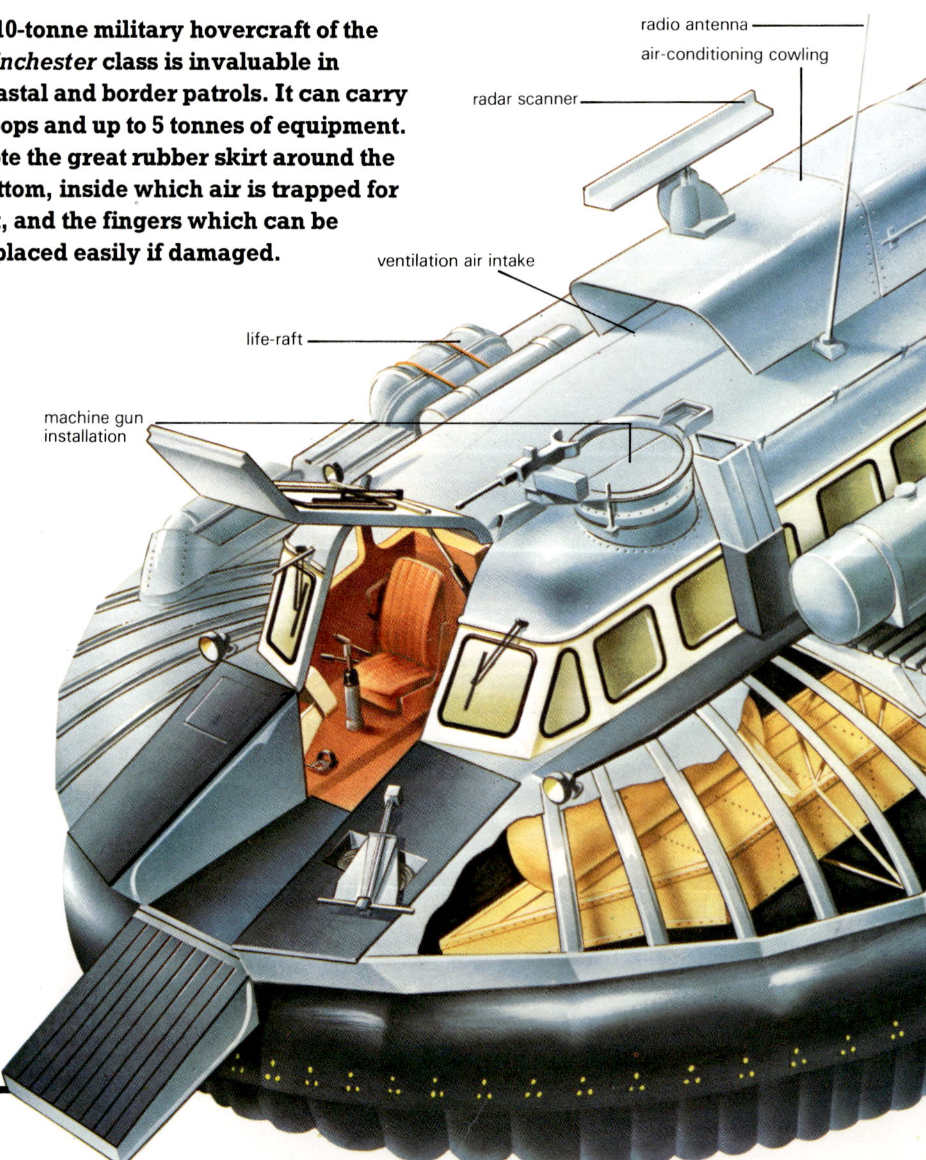

A 10-tonne military hovercraft of the *Winchester* class is invaluable in coastal and border patrols. It can carry troops and up to 5 tonnes of equipment. Note the great rubber skirt around the bottom, inside which air is trapped for lift, and the fingers which can be replaced easily if damaged.

cannot travel over rocky ground or wide ditches, or climb even moderately steep slopes. Because there is so little friction between the craft and surface, it is difficult to steer. It glides sideways with any tight turn and side winds blow it off course. If a wave kicks it up and a gust of wind gets underneath, then the whole craft may overturn. The

Right: The *Prince of Wales* SRN4 Mark 2 hovercraft built by the British Hovercraft Corporation. It has a top speed of 65 knots in calm weather.

SR.N6 Military Hovercraft

rides the wave crests.

The hovercraft principle has been applied to other things. The best example is the 'hovering' rotary blade lawnmower, where the engine creates a cushion of air within the casing and this raises the machine off the ground so that the blade always cuts at the same height. Heavy loads can be moved easily around a factory floor by inserting a 'hover-pallet' underneath, inflating it with a fan unit and then simply towing or pushing it around by hand. A road surface or bridge can be damaged or weakened by constant heavy traffic. But the modern air-cushion transporter spreads the load evenly and can carry up to 200 tonnes of cargo. Experimental air-cushion landing gear for aircraft is being investigated in the USA by Bell Aerospace. This would allow a large plane to land on swampy or icy surfaces, something a normal aircraft could not attempt.

Designers in the USSR are developing a new type of hovercraft, without the lift fans and the rubber skirt. It looks like an old-fashioned, twin-engined flying boat but with low-slung, short thick wings. The craft would be raised off the ground by its forward motion, with air cushions being created under the wings due to their aerodynamic design. Such craft could carry heavy loads for long distances on frozen rivers.

flexible rubber skirt can get damaged easily, passing over rough objects, and this cripples the craft since the air escapes from underneath and the hovercraft cannot lift off. And finally, a hovercraft is noisy and uncomfortable on long trips due to the noise of the propellers and the constant pitching and rolling as it

HYDROFOILS

A hydrofoil boat skims over the surface of the water at high speed. Wing-like structures, called hydrofoils, are attached to the hull and, out of water, the boat looks like it is on stilts. It is these hydrofoils that give the vessel its tremendous speed and smooth motion.

The development of these boats owes much to the science of aviation. In fact, hydrofoils act in exactly the same way as the aerofoils or wings of an airplane, except the first operate in water, the second in air. The principle is the same and is based on the physical law (called Bernoulli's Principle) that the faster a fluid or gas moves, the lower the pressure it exerts on objects over which it flows. This sounds complicated, but think of an aeroplane's wing. Its upper surface is curved and longer than the lower surface which is almost flat. As the plane moves forward, air rushes over the wing. It has to move further over the curved upper surface than the air passing beneath. So it moves faster and this makes for a lower pressure on the top of the wing. This difference in pressure causes the lift from below and so the plane takes off. The continual fast rush of air over the wings during flight maintains this lift and keeps the plane airborne.

In exactly the same way, a hydrofoil boat moves through the sea and water streams over and under the hydrofoil 'wings'. Since the water on the top curved surface is travelling further and faster than that on the bottom, there is lift from below and the boat is raised out of the water. The faster it moves, the more lift it gets.

Another major development in hydrofoil design also came from aviation technology. It is to do with the method of propulsion. Usually marine diesel engines give the forward thrust, by driving propellers at the end of long shafts; in the large military craft, gas turbines do the job. But, inspired by the way an aeroplane's jet engines suck in and expel air, designers introduced the water-jet system for hydrofoils. Here, the boat is propelled by thrust generated from the high-speed ejection of water. This led to the design of the modern Boeing *Jetfoil* passenger ferry in the early 1970s. Since 1975, *Jetfoil* ferries have skimmed across the Pearl River estuary every hour

Above: The basic hydrofoil design, supplied to the Royal Navy by Boeing, and modified by Vosper Thorneycroft.

Right: The Boeing *Jetfoil* in full flight, its hull well clear of the water, supported on struts.

Below: The hydrofoils below the hull act like underwater wings, giving lift. There are different designs. The submerged foils are automatically controlled and their angle varied according to wave conditions. The three surface-piercing designs allow the foils to break surface. When more lift is needed, the boat sinks lower.

between Hong Kong and Macau, a journey of 65 km (40 miles). They are double-decker, 27 m (90 ft)-long hydrofoils, with room for 350 passengers or 37 tonnes of cargo. They can cruise at a speed of 43 knots (80 km/h or 50 mph) in waves up to 4 m (12 ft) high. They are powered by high pressure water jet pumps, driven through reduction gearboxes by two gas turbine engines. Over 100,000 litres (23,000 gallons) of water are churned through the water pumps every minute.

In the development of hydrofoils, two main designs were conceived. Most commercial ferries, operating on fairly calm rivers or lakes, have the surface-piercing system. Here, the foils are V-shaped and part

of them is always above the water as the boat moves forward. When there is a loss of lift, the boat sinks a little in the water and the foils are immersed again to give more lift.

The second system is called the fully submerged hydrofoil and is used mainly by the military for naval craft in open sea. This design is more expensive and is controlled by an automatic electronic system. The foils are below water all the time. To keep the boat at a given height above the water, the amount of lift can be altered by varying the angle of the foils. A sonar device in the bow of the boat assesses the height of the oncoming waves and then selects the correct angle for the foils. This is transmitted by a hydraulic pressure system of rams

or rods connected directly to the foils. Gyroscopes in the hull also feed information to the computer to keep the boat level.

The world's largest hydrofoil with this design is the US Navy's *Plainview*. With a length of 64.6 m (212 ft) and a weight of 314 tonnes at full load, it has a service speed of 50 knots (92 km/h or 57 mph).

The sea-going, fully submerged hydrofoil boat had been proposed by two English brothers called Meacham back in the 1890s. But they were ahead of their time and the design had to wait for developments in computer technology and fluid dynamics. Then the German engineer Hans von Schertel finally cracked the design in the early 1960s, having been working on it since the '30s. Like so many other ventures, the military (especially the USA and Italy) became interested in the concept and invested in its development. The US *High Point* was the first fully submerged hydrofoil boat and came into service in 1963. It was built as a submarine chaser. The prototype for the water-jet propelled hydrofoil was the US *Tucumcari*, in 1968, from which the *Jetfoil* commercial ferry was developed. The Italian Navy's version of the water-jet hydrofoil is the *Sparviero*, which can carry guided missiles. It is now thought that hydrofoils the size of destroyers can soon be built, using some of the existing designs.

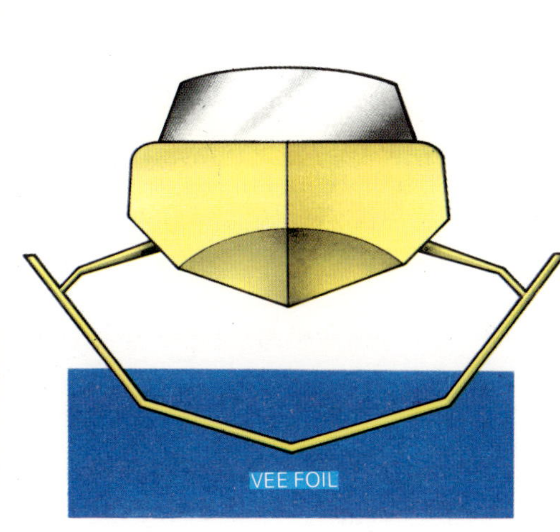

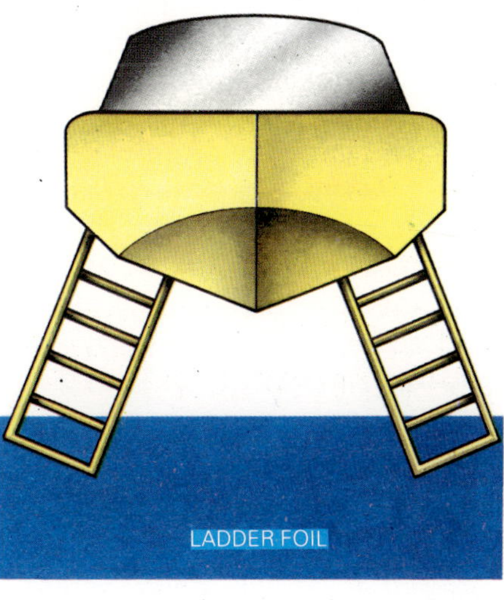

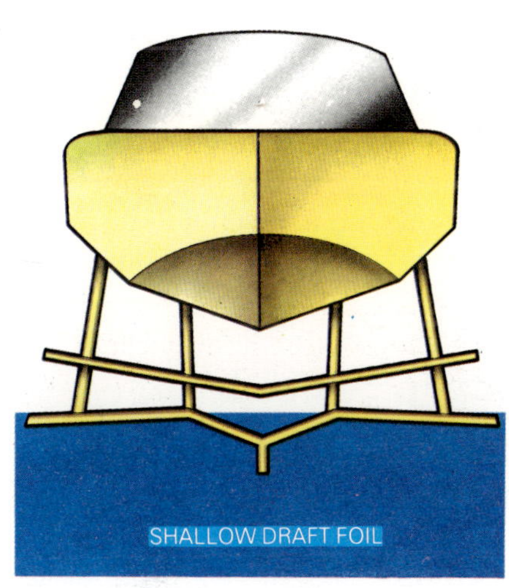

The revolution in the rapid transport of cargo by ships began in 1965 with the invention of the container — a strong, standard-sized, reusable, steel box containing the cargo. Today, giant container ships travel the world's shipping routes, each vessel carrying the equivalent cargo of up to seven conventional ships. Other giants roam the seas— oil tankers a quarter of a mile long and bulk carriers loaded with thousands of tons of grain.

Before the invention of the container ship, cargo came in all shapes and sizes, and had to be fitted into holds in the best way possible. Much time and effort was wasted trying to get the fit right. Costs were high to cover labour, packaging and insurance against damage. The ship would call to various ports (called 'break-bulking') until it had a full load. When it docked, days would be spent unloading. Such a ship would spend only 150 days of the year at sea. Compare this to a modern

container ship which spends 275 days a year at sea.

The simple idea of placing cargo in standardized containers and then loading these, with all cargoes assembled at one terminal, revolutionized merchant shipping. Great gantry cranes on the quayside, often with 36 m (120 ft)-long arms (booms), lift the containers aboard, loading one 35-ton crate every three minutes. (Compare the traditional method where it took one hour to load ten tons.) The ship's inside is divided into cells or separate holds.

The load capacity of a container ship is measured in units called TEUs. This means '20-foot equivalent units' and refers to the size of the container. Containers come in standard sizes, either 6 m (20 ft) or 12 m (40 ft) long. Thus a 12 m (40 ft) container represents 2 TEU. A modern ship can carry 2000 TEU comfortably, with a deadweight of 40,000 tonnes. The *Tokyo Bay* class of ship carries a

The largest ship in the world, the *Seawise Giant*, is also the largest tanker. Completed in 1979, it weighs over half a million tonnes and can carry half a million tonnes of oil, orange juice, grain, ore, in fact anything. It was fitted with an extra section in 1980 to make a total incredible length of 539 m (1770 ft).

load of 2600 TEU at a speed of 26 knots; the US *S1-7* travels at 33 knots with 2000 TEU. These great ships of the 1960s and '70s were powered by steam turbine engines, but in the '80s these are giving way to more economic, slower running diesels.

The world's largest container ship is the Japanese *Senshu Maru*. With a dead-weight of 106,500 tonnes, it is 283 m (928 ft) long with a beam of 45 m (147 ft).

Port Newark and Elizabeth in the USA is the world's leading container terminal port. It handles 9 million tons of cargo each year. Rotterdam handles some 4 million tons a year. The loading and off-

The world's largest moving machines, supertankers, need the world's largest propellers. This six-blader is 9.4 m (31 ft) in diameter and weighs 72 tonnes. It is fitted to the 386,000-ton tanker *Ioannis Coloctronis*.

Its decks loaded down, this container ship brings its valuable cargo from Hong Kong to Northern Europe in just 24 days average. Containers are stacked and locked together.

moving machines in the world. The great flat deck is almost two-thirds of the ship's length. It is built in sections so that a certain amount of 'give' or flexing can happen in rough seas which prevents the ship from breaking up. The engines, bridge and cabins are located at the stern, where there is a double bottom to the hull for extra strength. Oil is pumped directly into the loading tanks and each tank is separated from the next in case of leakage. Should one tank be holed, the ship will not sink due to these watertight compartments. Another advantage of separate tanks is that different types of oils can be carried without mixing.

The supertankers are called Ultra Large Crude Carriers (ULCC) and can transport up to half a million tons of oil. The *Batillus* is a ULCC and is so large that it needs two steam turbine engines and two five-bladed propellers, each weighing 52 tons, to drive it. There are also two rudders for steering. All tankers are computer-controlled. Great care is needed in handling oil at all stages, but especially when loading in case the weight of oil puts too much stress on any one part of the ship's structure which would cause it to break in half.

LASH (Lighter Aboard Ship) is another form of cargo ship, although this time the 'cargo' is other smaller boats called 'lighters'. These are loaded with cargo but have no engines. Several of them are pulled by tug to the mother LASH ship where they are then floated aboard into its holds. At the end of the trip, the lighters are towed away, up rivers and canals, to deliver their cargoes.

The *Seabee* was the first LASH. This type of ship could carry 26 lighters, each displacing 1300 tonnes loaded, stowed on three levels. But an enormous electrically powered lifting platform was needed to raise the lighters aboard. In the modern LASH, for example the Japanese *Mammoth Oak*, the lighters are floated aboard to fit snugly in the holds.

loading operations are controlled by computer and a central network links all container ports worldwide.

Another form of containerized shipping is the Ro-Ro (roll-on, roll-off) system, where 30–40-ton loaded trailers drive onto the ship for a short sea trip, such as between the UK and the Continent. The American *El Rey* barge is the largest Ro-Ro ship in the world. It weighs some 16,700 tonnes and is 177 m (580 ft) long. Up to 376 truck-trailers are housed on three levels and the ship operates between Florida and Puerto Rico.

The first oil tanker, the *Gluckauf*, was built in England in 1886 for a German owner. Since then, oil tankers have become the largest

SAIL RETURNS

The old days of sail are gone, except for pleasure craft and naval training ships. The idea of transporting commercial cargo around the world these days in sailing ships—along busy shipping lanes, at the mercy of winds and currents—is unthinkable. It would take too long, and therefore be uneconomic, and it could also be dangerous. And yet, the fact is sail *is* returning, but in combination with modern engines. Here, we have the best of both worlds. The economic and environmental advantages of wind—it is free and there is no pollution; and the overriding consideration in today's world where oil, coal and other natural resources are becoming scarce, if not exhausted—wind energy may cut a ship's fuel costs by half.

So far, there are not many of these sailing cargo ships in use. In 1980, Japan launched the world's first sail-assisted commercial tanker, the *Shin Aituko Maru*. Germany, Britain and the USA are developing new designs and models.

The *Shin Aituko Maru* is a strange-looking ship. Its 'sails' are rigid and mounted on two masts, for and aft. They are controlled by a computer on the bridge, which sets their angle to the wind. When the wind direction changes, this is sensed by the computer and the sails are adjusted accordingly. Each sail is made of a fixed centre panel and two side panels that can be folded back, like the wings of a butterfly, when not in use. When spread, each sail measures 12 m high and 8 m wide (40 × 6 ft). With a 30-knot wind blowing on the beam (side),

the ship can make 15 knots headway on its sails alone. (Compare a modern powered lifeboat, built for speed and racing to the scene of an emergency, which travels at 18 knots.) A diesel engine of only 1600 hp is installed, a much smaller than normal engine for such a large tanker. It can be used in harness with the sails or it can provide power only to manoeuvre the ship in an awkward space, such as a harbour, in an emergency, or when there is no wind blowing.

The Japanese spent 2.3 million dollars building the *Shin Aituko Maru*, about half a million more than a conventional tanker. But they are confident that the cost will be repaid many times over, because fuel savings of 50% are expected. In addition, it is claimed that a crew of only eight can handle the ship, thus cutting down on manpower costs.

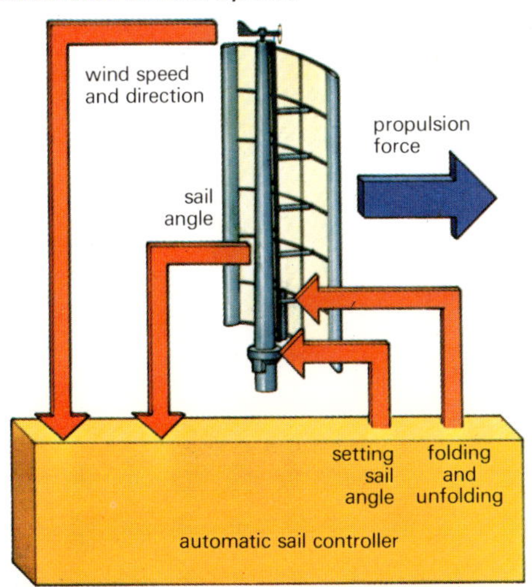

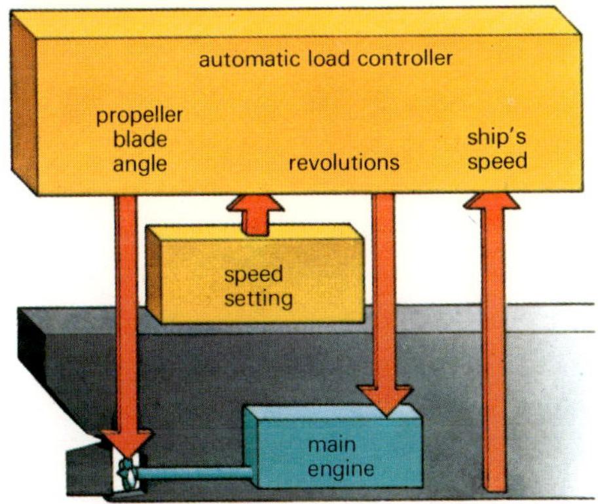

Left: The automatic control system of the *Shin Aituko Maru* is simplicity itself, at least for a computer. A series of transducers in the masts feeds information to the central computer about changes in wind direction and speed, and the sails are 'set' (angled) automatically for maximum wind power. Output of the main engine is modified so a set speed is maintained. Right: The real thing: a traditionally designed sailing ship, the US barque *Eagle* is a splendid sight in full sail entering harbour during the 1972 Tall Ships race.

As an experiment in economics and environmental care, the Japanese have led the way.

The German *Dynaship* is at the experimental stage. It is a modern version of the traditional square-rigged windjammer. Like its old counterpart, the *Dynaship* carries dozens of sails—30 in fact, five on each of the six giant masts placed the length of the deck. The masts are set in revolving bases and so the whole structure, mast and sail, can be automatically turned to the wind, controlled by computer. The sails can be stowed away easily by reeling them into slots in the hollow masts. Again, this is done automatically. The result of this

Left: The world's first sail-assisted commercial ship, the *Shin Aituko Maru* is seen in full sail and with sails folded (above). A revolution in modern design, it draws on the oldest sailing power in the world—wind. With its modest engine, savings of almost 50% can be made on its fuel bills.

great mass of sail, over 5000 square meters (16,500 sq ft) in area, is that the *Dynaship* can exceed 20 knots in a 35-knot wind.

The British version is called the *Sailiner* and has been on the drawing board since 1977. With a displacement of 12,000 tonnes, she is a large, wind-propelled, steel-hulled, diesel-engined windjammer. In theory, it has been estimated that the *Sailiner* could sail, under wind power alone, from England to Melbourne, Australia, and back again, via the Cape of Good Hope, in 104 days. The same journey, by engine-powered vessel, and shortcutting through the Suez Canal, would take 82 days. This is a somewhat shorter time but the *Sailiner*'s savings in fuel could be as much as 90%, well worth the extra 22 days.

One of the problems still to be solved in the German and UK design is that the great mass of rigid sail, rigging and numerous thick masts clutter up the deck and get in

the way of loading and off-loading cargo. The many advantages, however, of these super-sailing ships would seem to outweigh the few disadvantages.

There are several new ideas being developed today for sail-assisted trading ships. One involves wind-power using aerofoils. These are made of a flexible, double-skin fabric and can be reefed, concertina-fashion, in strong winds. Experiments in a wind tunnel, with a model comparable in bulk to the *Dynaship*, have indicated that speeds of 15 knots could be achieved in a 20-knot, beam-on wind. A great advantage is that such aerofoil sails can point to within 60° of the wind (not too far off sailing into it) before tacking, or turning the ship, is necessary.

Another idea proposes that wind-power be harnessed by great turbines on deck, to generate thrust and move the ship upwind, using engines only in an emergency or when there is insufficient wind.

CHAPTER 4

INDUSTRIAL MACHINES

We live in a highly mechanized society. An increasing world population makes more and more demands on our resources and on our ability to use these resources. From basic tools to help man's labour, industry has developed sophisticated machines to allow larger and more complex tasks to be completed.

Precise handling of giant structures, giant digging and boring Supermachines, and robot conrol of simpler machines have extended our ability to shape our environment. We must be careful not to abuse this power.

In the future our most complex machines will become simpler to use as computer control becomes ever more common.

Industry provides us with the true giants of the Supermachine world.

This gigantic bucket-wheel excavator is extracting thousands of tonnes of gold-bearing ore from a quarry in Russia.

THE CRANE

The huge structures and machines built by man could not be constructed without the use of cranes. Cranes capable of lifting up to 3000 tonnes in a single load have been constructed. An enormous variety of shapes and sizes of crane exist, depending on the special role for which they have been designed. Many cranes are fixed or can be moved only with difficulty—but large road going cranes, able to travel quickly to various sites, have an important role to play.

Cantilever, or tower, cranes are used to perform heavy lifting duties in shipbuilding and in the construction of large buildings. They consist of a tall vertical lattice work tower with a jib supported at 90° to the tower, making a T shape.

A large counterweight is attached to one shortened arm of the jib. The lifting cables are attached to a trolley which can travel along the other arm of the jib. The cantilever crane is capable of lifting up to 150 tonnes and accurately positioning the load anywhere on the site within reach of the jib.

Useful as these cranes are they have to be transported to the site in sections and erected with the aid of another crane. One of the cranes capable of doing this job is the Coles *Hydra Truck*.

ROAD CRANES

The Coles *Hydra Truck* and other similar cranes are self propelled, telescopic jib cranes with about a 45 tonne lifting capacity.

Having travelled to the site by road, the crane puts out extension side arms and lowers hydraulic jacks to the ground to provide a firm lifting base. A fly jib is then swung into place as an extension to the main jib and hydraulic rams raise the jib to its working position. The jib telescopes out to its full length and the crane lifts.

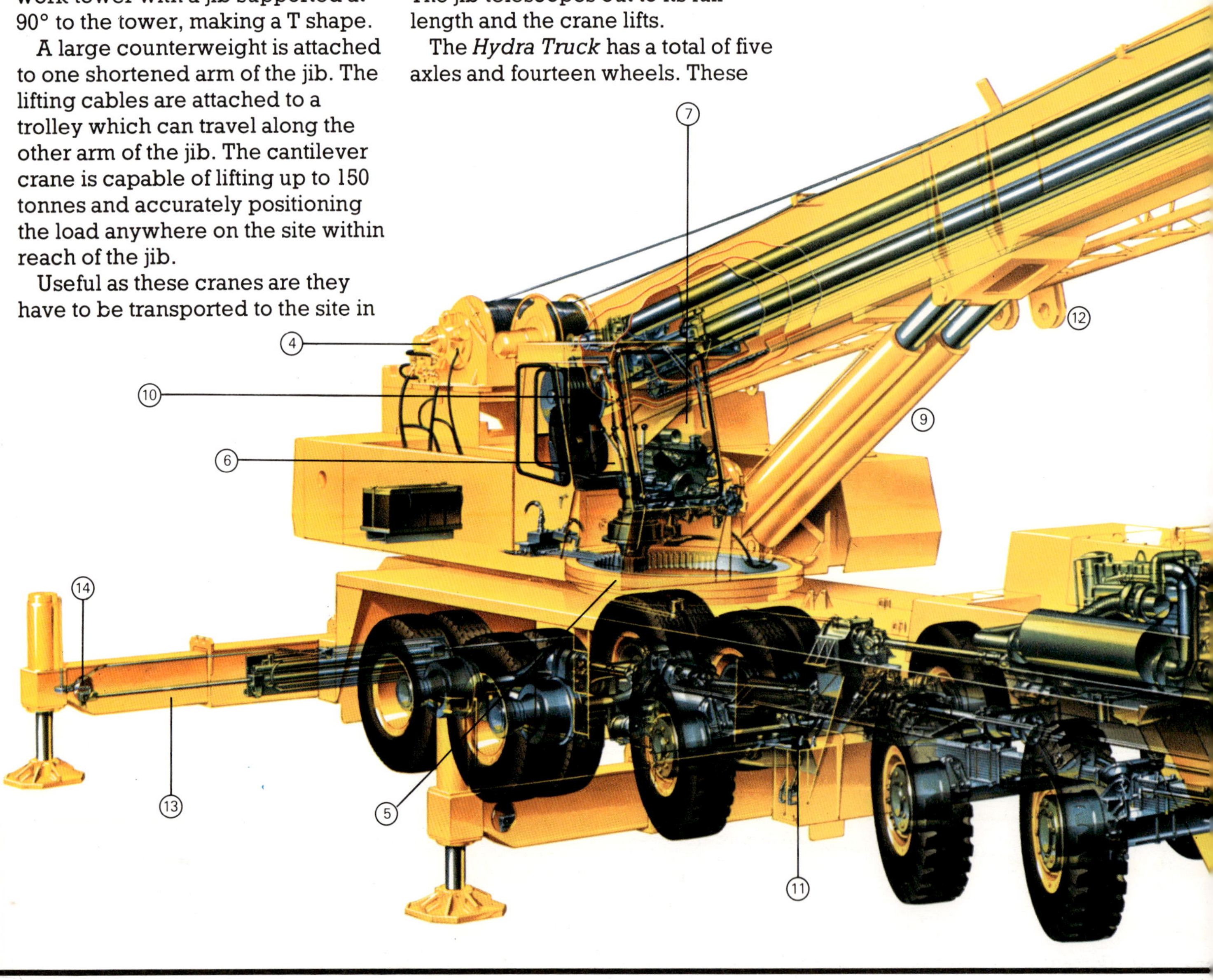

The *Hydra Truck* has a total of five axles and fourteen wheels. These

are necessary to support the weight of the counterweights that the crane needs to carry in order to be stable under load. The driver's and crane operator's cabs are comfortably upholstered and air conditioned.

Left: An articulated arm mounted on a railway truck is being used here to inspect the underside of a rail bridge. Previously this would have required scaffolding and might have meant the closure of tracks.

Road cranes capable of lifting loads of up to 1000 tonnes have been built. Cranes for use on rough terrain have metal tracks.

ACCESS PLATFORMS

The use of hydraulics in cranes has led to the development of articulated crane arms. These can bend at the joints of the arms to allow access to difficult areas. If the head of the crane arm is replaced by a platform, men can inspect or work in areas that previously would have required complicated and dangerous scaffolding to be erected. Work can be speeded up and more regular inspection take place.

Articulated arms are regular sights on the roads where they are used to service streetlamps and overhead traffic signs. Rail mounted articulated access platforms are now being used to inspect the underside of bridges and viaducts —a job that would previously take several days work can now be completed in a few hours.

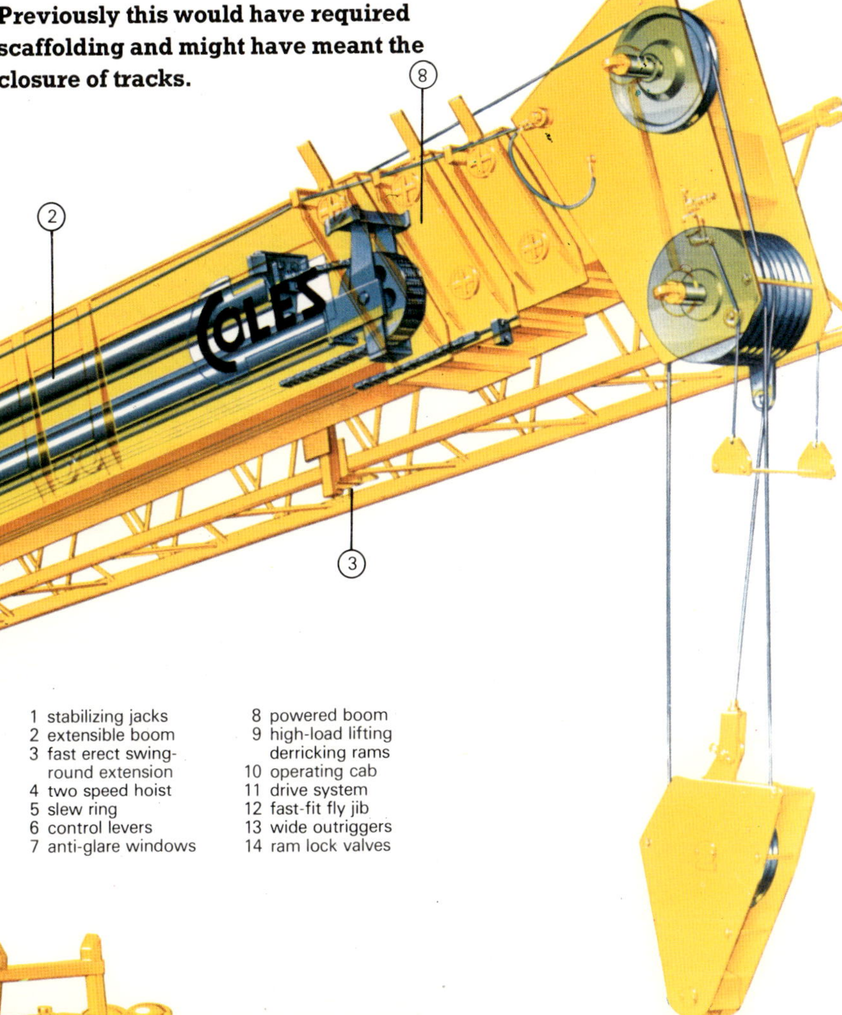

1 stabilizing jacks
2 extensible boom
3 fast erect swing-round extension
4 two speed hoist
5 slew ring
6 control levers
7 anti-glare windows
8 powered boom
9 high-load lifting derricking rams
10 operating cab
11 drive system
12 fast-fit fly jib
13 wide outriggers
14 ram lock valves

Left: A Coles *Hydra Truck* road going crane puts supports in preparation for extending the telescopic jib. Self contained and self powered, the crane can place heavy machinery inside factories through the roof.

Right: The jib of a large road crane fully extended. The telescopic sections are octagonal for extra strength.

GIANT EXCAVATORS

Open cast (surface) mines need giant excavators to extract the large amounts of coal required by industry. Two very different types of Supermachine help perform this task. Bucket wheel excavators tear away at the coal and carry it away on conveyer belts, and the giant walking draglines scoop out enormous buckets full of the covering overburden of shale, sand, limestone or gravel to reveal the coal seams.

THE WALKING DRAGLINE

The greatest asset of the walking dragline is its enormous reach and capacity. A typical walking dragline can move up to 4500 tonnes of overburden in an hour. The largest walking dragline, *Big Muskie* (which works in the Muskingham mine at Cumberland, Ohio), can shift up to 10,000 tonnes in an hour. A typical dragline has a bucket capacity of about 100 cu m (145 cu yds) and a boom of about 120 m (400 ft). The electric motors which power the dragline can be up to 13,500 kw (18,090 hp) in capacity.

A walking dragline gets its name from the way it moves about the site. On either side of the dragline are large metal 'shoes'. When the dragline is moved it is first raised on these 'shoes' so that the main body is clear of the ground. The main body then slides forwards a short distance and the body is then lowered to the ground. As the process is repeated the dragline slowly moves forwards in a process that can best be described as walking.

To operate the scoop bucket it is first lowered to the ground on the hoist ropes. The drag ropes are then winched in and the front of the bucket digs into the soil scooping it up as the bucket moves towards the main body of the dragline. When the bucket is full it is lifted on the hoist ropes while the drag ropes are played out to prevent the contents from spilling. The jib can then be swung to any position and the useless contents dumped.

Extensive walkways are provided for maintenance and inspection of the jib. A dragline normally operates with a crew of three, one controlling from the cab, one in the motor room, and one outside to ensure safety on the site.

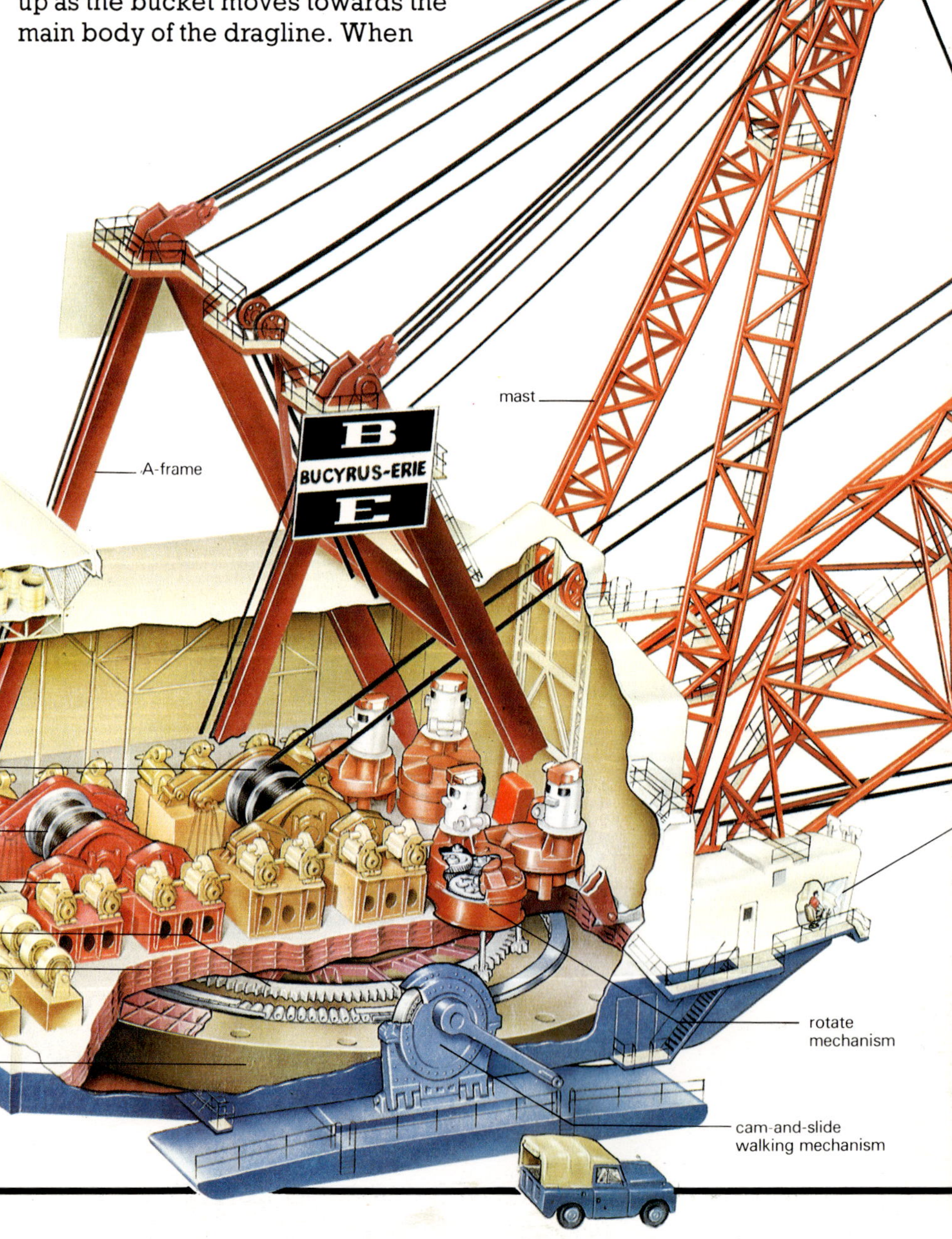

THE BUCKET-WHEEL EXCAVATOR

The bucket-wheel excavator is able to perform the task of shifting the overburden from above coal seams but, because it uses smaller buckets with a sharp edge, it can also extract the coal directly.

These giant excavators can weigh up to 7500 tonnes and be up to 200 m (656 ft) long and 70 m (230 ft) high. Worked by a crew of five these machines can remove more than 8400 cu m (90,385 cu ft) of coal in one hour.

The coal is removed along a conveyer belt to waiting trains or lorries. The cutting head and conveyer belt are both positioned

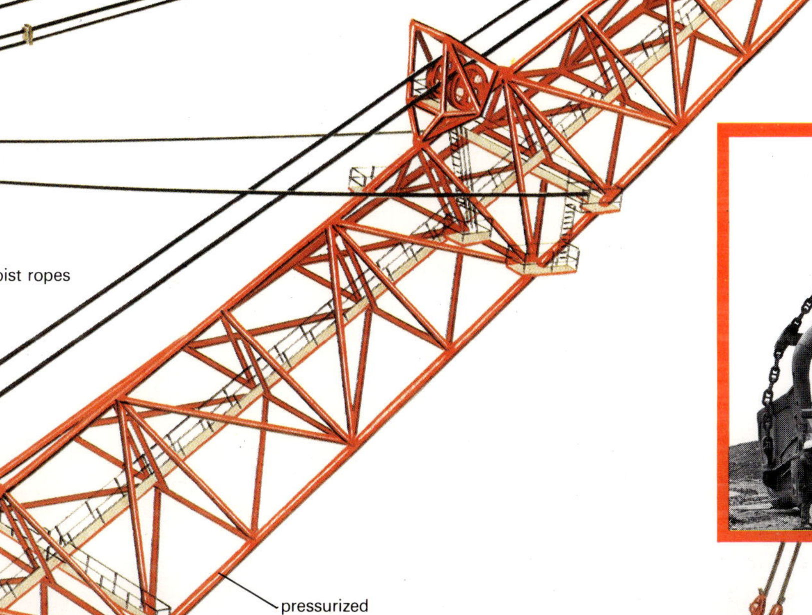

Above: A dragline capable of lifting 10–12 tonnes in its bucket sits inside the bucket of *Big Geordie*, the largest walking dragline in Europe.

Left: A section through a large walking dragline. One of the large walking 'shoes' can be clearly seen at the side of the main body.

Below left: A giant bucket-wheel excavator at work in the Fortuna mine in West Germany. Several such excavators work on the same site.

by a powerful jib and the excavator moves on metal caterpillar tracks.

The coal that is extracted from open-cast mines is generally of much lower quality than that found in underground mines.

For an open-cast mine to be economical it must be large—giant excavators are the only practical way of working these large mines.

GOING UNDERGROUND

Man uses tunnels for many purposes today—for underground train services in cities, for road and rail tunnels through mountains and under rivers, and to carry water in hydro-electric power schemes.

Originally all these tunnels had to be dug by hand. The process was speeded up with the introduction of blasting techniques. Now new super tunnelling machines make this task much simpler, faster and safer—whether the tunnel is being bored through soft mud or rock.

Once a tunnel has been bored it is lined with metal or concrete shields to help support and waterproof the walls. The modern tunnelling machine can line the tunnel with shields at the same time as it is cutting its way through the rock.

Tunnel Boring Machines (or TBMs) use either full faced blades for tunnelling through soft materials such as clay, or hardened rotary cutters which grind and reduce hard materials such as granite to a fine powder.

TBMs can weigh over 300 tonnes and cut tunnels up to 10 m (33 ft) in

Below: A section through a modern tunnel boring machine. In this case a full face blade is being used to cut through soft material. The concrete tunnel linings can be seen in place along the completed tunnel walls.

diameter. Tremendous power is required to apply enough thrust to the rock face. Motors of 1500 to 2200 kw (2000 to 3000 hp) are used.

Right: A 'jumbo' percussive drilling machine with four hydraulic drill arms and two inspection platform arms.

Below: A tunnel boring machine completing a shaft at the hydro-electric power station at Mapragg in Switzerland.

Special pressure lubricated bearings are used in the cutting head to withstand the heavy loads to which it is subjected.

The cutter heads are thrust against the rock face by large and powerful hydraulic rams. In the case of the largest tunnellers this force can be over 1.1 million

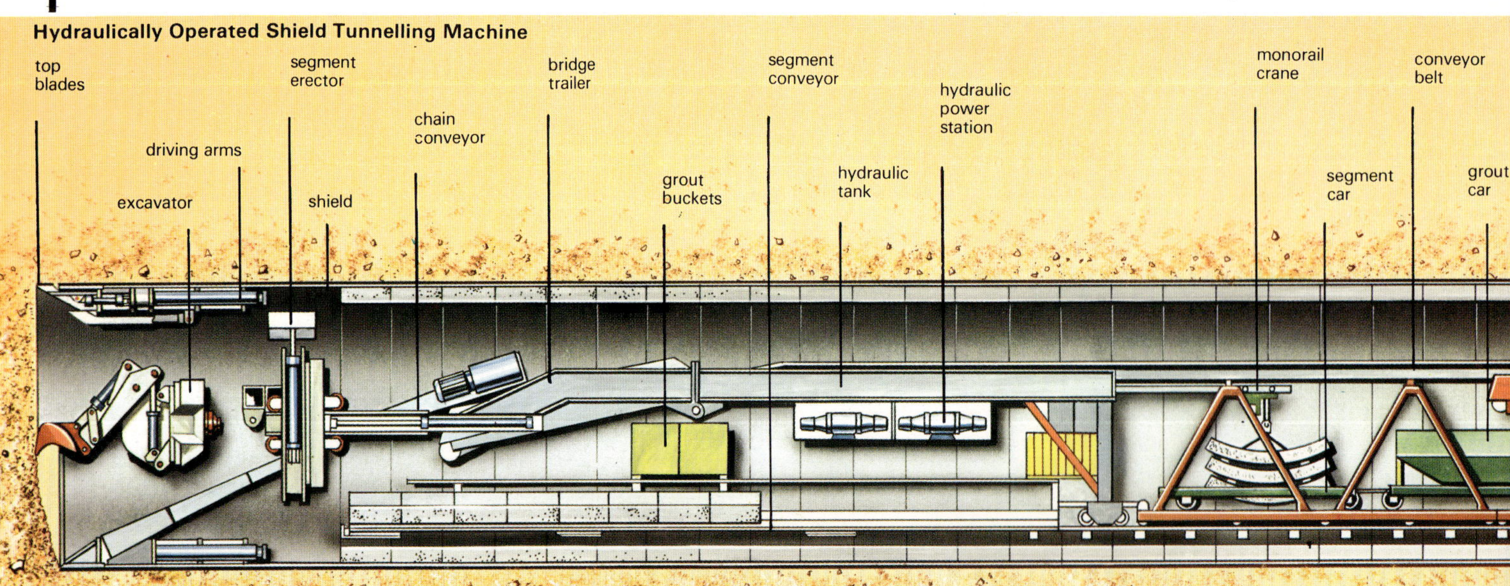

kilogrammes (2.5 million pounds). Other hydraulic rams push against the walls of the tunnel to support and stabilize the cutting head.

Although the machine is designed to cut straight tunnels a limited amount of steering is possible and with the aid of a laser guidance system curved tunnels can be cut.

The crushed rock produced by the rotary cutters falls to the base of the cutting head and is scooped onto a conveyer belt. It is then carried along the inside of the cutting machine to a waiting train of muck cars which are hauled along a track back to the surface by a battery powered locomotive.

Following the progress of the cutting head shield segments are fed forwards and are manoeuvred into position on the tunnel walls by a special hydraulic device. They are then cemented in place and the tunnel walls sealed.

While tunnelling compressed air is fed into the tunnel to prevent water seeping out of the unsealed walls and flooding the tunnel. The compressed air also reduces the risk of the tunnel walls crumbling. Any miners working in the tunnel need to undergo decompression (just like deep sea divers) before they can return to the surface.

Although the TBM represents a major advance in tunnel boring, over 80% of tunnels are still cut using explosives placed in carefully positioned holes in the rock face.

The latest type of drill used to cut the holes for the charges is the electro-hydraulic hammer or percussive drill. A piston is pushed forwards hydraulically and strikes the drill rod shank. Energy is then transmitted to the tungsten carbide drill tip in the form of a shock wave strong enough to crush rock.

A number of these drills mounted on hydraulic booms are placed on a large wheeled vehicle which is known as a 'jumbo'. Once the correct number of charge holes have been cut in the rock face explosives are placed in them and a detonator attached. After the explosion clearing vehicles can pass underneath the body of the 'jumbo' to remove the rubble.

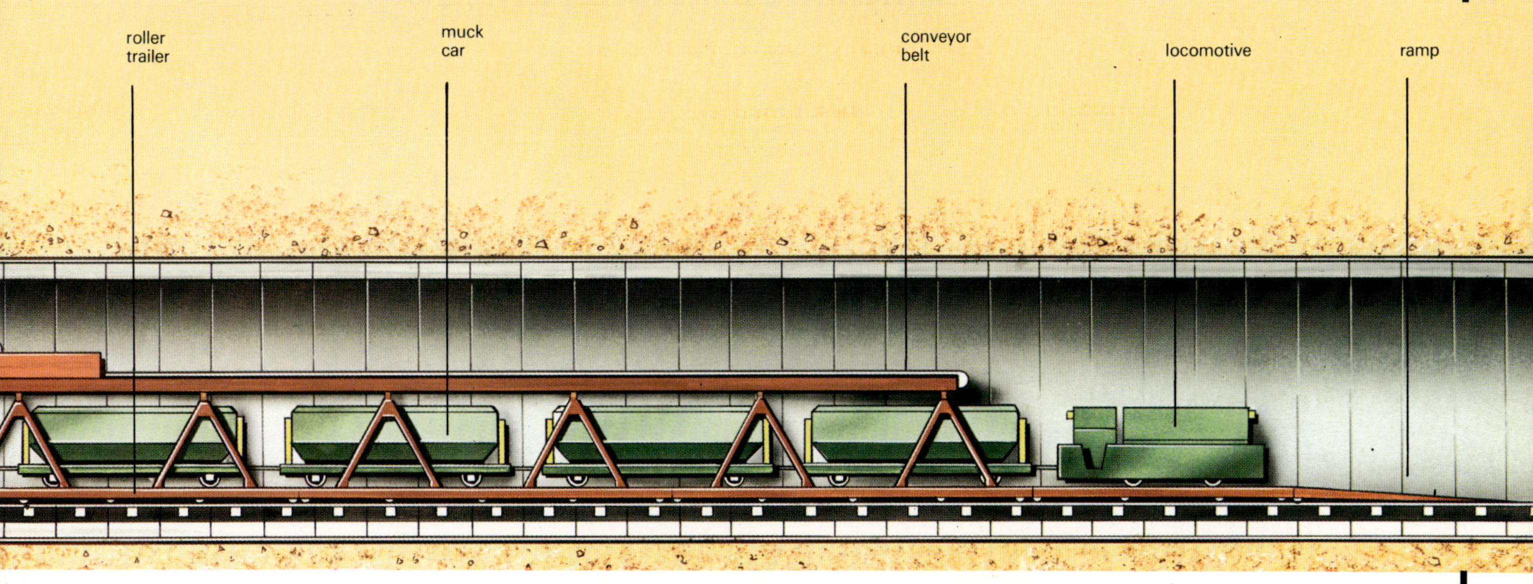

ROBOT & SIMULATOR

The popular view of robots is that of the almost human machines seen in films such as *Star Wars*. These multitasking intelligent beings can walk and talk and are really used as domestic servants. This image is far from the reality of the industrial robot.

The industrial robot is a machine which is designed to move tools and parts through a range of preplanned movements in order to perform a specific job.

The limited memory of the industrial robot is programmed to perform the same operation over and over again. Their main use is to take over boring and repetitive tasks from human beings.

Once a robot has been 'taught' how to paint a car or weld two parts together it will go on doing this job until instructed to stop. Factories that are equipped totally with robots can work twenty-four hours a day with no rest breaks.

An automated assembly track in a car factory can take in all the component parts of the car, weld together sections of the body, paint it, fit the engine and transmission, the doors and windows, and all the wiring and electrical equipment. Robot trucks move the sections of car between the various assembly lines and at the end of the process a completed car emerges from the factory—all with no human intervention.

The most common type of industrial robot consists of an hydraulically powered arm with articulated joints and a hand which can grip and lift objects. Feedback can make the hand sensitive enough to pick up eggs without breaking them or strong enough to lift very heavy weights.

Robots are also very useful for work in hazardous environments such as at the bottom of the ocean or in space. Special sensors can be fitted to allow the detection of gases or dangerous chemicals.

In the future more sophisticated robots will be constructed to

Above: Robots at work welding on a car assembly line.

Right: A pilot at the controls of an aircraft flight simulator is about to make a night time landing approach to a computer generated runway.

perform more complicated tasks. At the moment robots are only at an early stage in their development. Much more work is needed on the devices that are used by robots to sense the world around them. The computers that control them have to become more sophisticated, smaller and be programmed in such a way that they have an artificial intelligence. In this way robots will be more able to perform complicated tasks and to learn from their own experience.

SIMULATORS

Aeroplanes, ships and space vehicles are complicated and expensive machines. Training crew to operate these vehicles is a long and dangerous procedure.

Now computer and robot technologies have made it possible to simulate all the movements and behaviour of a real vehicle without ever leaving the training room.

A flight simulator consists of an exact replica of the inside of the control room or cockpit of the real vehicle. All controls look and feel like the real thing. All the usual sounds will be relayed to the inside of the cockpit. Outside, and visible through the windows, is a projected realistic computer model of the world as it would be seen from inside the real aeroplane at any time in the flight. At the beginning of a session it will show the particular airport scene where the flight is due to start from.

This cockpit model sits on a motion base which consists of a number of hydraulic rams which are linked to a computer to accurately reproduce the motion of the flight. If there is a rough landing the crew will certainly feel it.

Controllers sitting outside the simulator are able to programme

Above: Two flight simulators on their motion bases help train Lufthansa flight crews in their training centre.

Right: This science fiction robot from the film *Star Wars* is in the process of repairing its own leg.

into the computer any possible combination of events. Bad visibility, failing engines and other equipment, severe turbulence and even ice on the runway can be simulated in a way that is all too real for the training crew members.

Delays in the response of the controls of the real craft are reproduced accurately in the simulator and it is even possible to use the simulator to predict how the craft would behave in given circumstances.

A number of airlines are now conducting most of their flight crew training on simulators. It is possible that the first time that a pilot actually flies the real aeroplane it will be with fare paying passengers.

Helicopters, oil tankers, submarines and space vehicles are among the growing number of uses for total environment simulators. These machines are very expensive at the moment but soon we may see simulators taking over for car driving instruction.

CHAPTER 5

FLIGHT

People have dreamed of flying since the earliest of times, but it was not until the year 1783 that a hot air balloon designed by the Montgolfier brothers in France first carried Man into the skies.

The development of heavier-than-air craft could not take place until lightweight and powerful engines were first developed.

On 17 December 1903 the *Flyer*, built and piloted by the Wright brothers in the USA, made the first aeroplane flight.

Since then aeroplanes have developed into the Supermachines of today—capable of flying faster than sound, of carrying hundreds of passengers, and even of flying backwards.

The elegant engineering of the supersonic airliner *Concorde* seen at the point of take off.

THE JUMBO

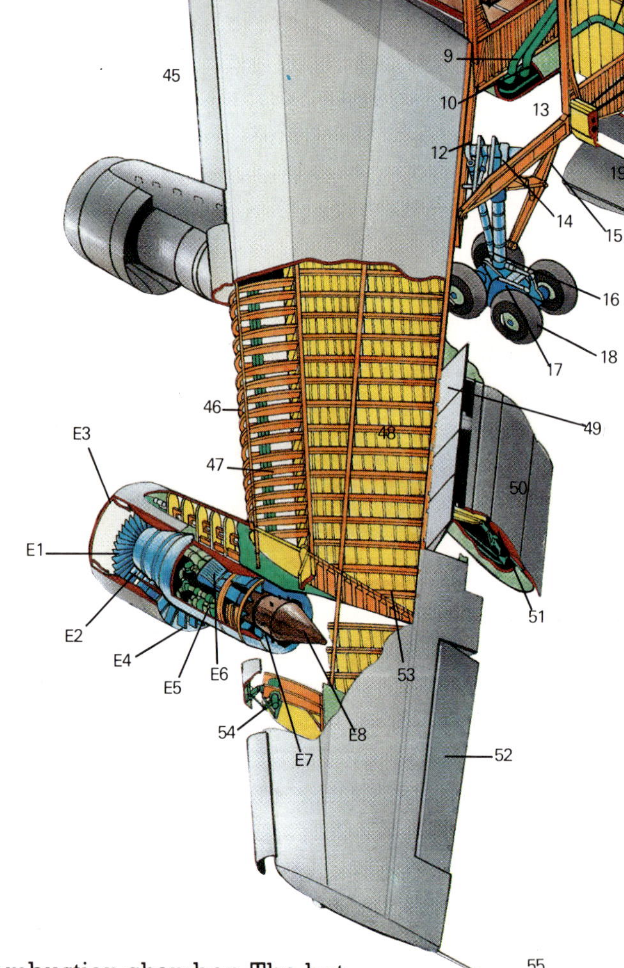

fan operates at lower speeds than in a standard turbojet engine less unpleasant noise is produced.

The passengers on a *Jumbo* sit in rows of up to ten seats across the body of the aeroplane, while standard jet aeroplanes are only wide enough for four or five seats.

The *Jumbo* is double decked

As the aeroplane developed into a more reliable and faster machine it began to be used to carry passengers. Twin piston engined and fully enclosed aircraft carrying up to thirty passengers were in service in the 1930s.

Seaplanes made longer journeys across the sea possible with frequent refuelling stops. Eventually the aeroplane took over from the ocean going liner as the popular method of crossing the Atlantic.

With the development of the jet engine, speeds, range and reliability increased. As flying became more easily accessible more and more people wanted to fly. By the time the *Jumbo* was first developed in 1970 it had become possible to carry up to 500 passengers in one aeroplane.

THE BOEING 747

The Boeing 747 *Jumbo* was the first of a new generation of the wide bodied aeroplanes which could carry large passenger loads in comfort and safety.

The *Jumbo* is powered by four large turbofan engines which are designed to be both quieter and more efficient than the standard jet turbine engine. It operates with a flight crew of three.

A large fan driven by the turbine of the jet engine blows air not only into but also around the engine providing both thrust and cooling. In the engine the air is compressed further and then mixed with fuel in

a combustion chamber. The hot exhaust gases, produced by the burning fuel, drive turbine blades to power the compressor blades and the fan through a reduction gearbox. The exhaust gases also provide thrust to drive the aeroplane forwards. Because the

The Boeing 747-200 *Jumbo* passenger jet liner was first flown on 11 October 1970. The increased efficiency and passenger carrying capacity led to a significant reduction in travel costs over existing airliners. The large turbofan engines resulted in a reduction in noise generated on take-off and landing.

with a lounge above the 1st class passenger section which is reached via a spiral staircase. In some extended capacity *Jumbos* there are also additional passenger seats on the top deck.

Passengers are able to watch

inflight films or listen to one of several different sound programmes. As with all modern airliners, meals and drinks are served during the flight. The reclining seats are designed to be comfortable throughout long flights.

Climbing to a height of about

weight on take-off is 377,850 kg (833,000 lb).

Now designs are being considered for a version of the *Jumbo* with a full upper deck and a seating capacity of over 650.

Engine Details
E1 fan
E2 stators
E3 air door inlets
E4 by-pass
E5 manifolding
E6 cooler
E7 thrust reversers
E8 thrust cone

1 glass fibre radar cone
2 flight engineer's seat
3 flt eng's electronics panel
4 staircase to . . .
5 upper first class lounge
6 forward passenger door
7 body frames
8 main frames
9 body bulkhead
10 engine start air (from APU)
11 load bearing floor
12 rear spar
13 undercarriage beam
14 retraction jacks
15 breaker strut actuator
16 main strut

17 brake reaction link
18 low profile tyres
19 undercarriage door
20 hot air manifold
21 keel box
22 centre keel
23 centre section fairing
24 centre passenger door
25 air conditioning ducts
26 galley
27 floor spars
28 freight floor
29 freight hold door
30 rear door
31 crew wardrobe
32 toilets
33 rear pressure bulkhead
34 tailplane incidence jack
35 tailplane frames
36 light alloy sheet skin
37 fin front section box
38 fin torsion box
39 static discharge wicks
40 two piece rudder
41 two piece elevator
42 auxiliary power unit (APU)
43 APU air inlets
44 navigation light
45 leading edge flap
46 leading edge ribs
47 leading edge flap drives
48 main torsion box (fuel tank)

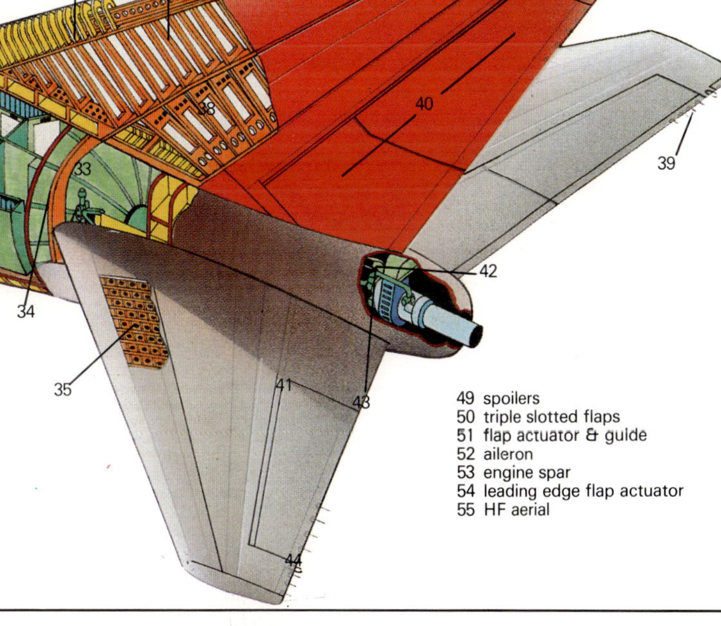

49 spoilers
50 triple slotted flaps
51 flap actuator & guide
52 aileron
53 engine spar
54 leading edge flap actuator
55 HF aerial

10,670 metres (35,000 ft) the *Jumbo* can cruise at a speed of about 898 km/h (558 mph) to cross the Atlantic Ocean, from London to New York in about seven hours.

THE 747-300

The latest version of the *Jumbo* is the 747-300. This aeroplane is an extended version of the original aircraft. It first flew in 1982 and is capable of carrying 484 passengers in economy class seating on the lower deck and 69 passengers sitting six abreast on the upper deck. Powered by four Pratt & Whitney JT9D-74G2 turbofans it has a maximum range of 13,850 km (8606 miles).

The wing span of the aircraft is 59.64 m (195 ft 8 in) and its length 70.51 m (231 ft 4 in). The maximum

Fact file . . .

The first commercial jet airliner was the de Havilland Comet which was built in Great Britain in 1949.

When the first tests of the *Shuttle* were taking place in the USA it was carried into the air on the back of a converted *Jumbo* before being launched.

CONCORDE

Concorde was born from an Anglo-French agreement made in 1962 to jointly develop a supersonic airliner to cater for business men and women, who were becoming ever-more frequent travellers, so that they might waste less time in the air. A supersonic airliner could cut the flight time from London to New York to just over three hours. The cost would always be higher than for slower economically-built airliners carrying many more passengers but it was judged that the need for speed was there.

The first prototype *Concorde* took off on 2 March 1969 in France and the second on 9 April of the same year in England.

Design considerations are very different for aeroplanes flying above the speed of sound.

The engines of the *Concorde* are four Rolls Royce/Snecma Olympus afterburning 593 turbojets each producing 17,260 kg (38,050 lb) thrust. The engines are slim turbojets for efficiency at supersonic speeds. To increase thrust on take-off fuel is injected into the stream of exhaust gases as they emerge from the turbine and burnt (afterburning).

The wings of the *Concorde* are specially designed to give good lift at both subsonic and supersonic speeds. The particular shape of wing used is called an ogival delta.

The fuselage is necessarily slim in relation to the length of the aeroplane. In fact only four passenger seats can be fitted across the fuselage. The aeroplane wings and fuselage are painted white to help disperse the extra heat that is produced in supersonic flight. The maximum speed of the aeroplane is limited more by its ability to withstand heat than by power considerations. Some military aeroplanes can fly much faster than *Concorde* for short periods but must slow down to prevent their metal skins from melting.

The shape of *Concorde*'s fuselage limits seating to a maximum of 144 plus three crew. The maximum take-off weight of *Concorde* is 185,065 kg (407,994 lb), with a maximum range of 6228 km (3870 miles). The empty seat to weight ratio is three times that of the *Jumbo*, making it a much more expensive aeroplane to fly.

Although *Concorde* is capable of flying at mach 2.04 (just over twice the speed of sound) it has to fly at subsonic speeds for much of its journey over land because supersonic flight causes an unpleasant sonic boom.

The combination of high operating costs and noise problems at take-off and landing has meant

The USAF XB-70 experimental supersonic aeroplane could have become a supersonic airliner but the project was abandoned. The latest proposals are for hypersonic craft.

that only sixteen *Concorde*s plus prototypes were ever produced. Of these, seven are flying with British Airways and seven with Air France. These *Concorde*s are now operating at a trading profit and there is talk of producing a second generation.

Both the Americans and Russians have made attempts to produce a supersonic airliner. The American project was abandoned early and the experimental XB-70 is used only for military development.

The Russian Tupolev *Tu-144* which looks very similar to *Concorde*, in fact flew before *Concorde* in 1968.

Above: One of British Airways' fleet of *Concordes*, an elegant but expensive means of travel.

Below: A prototype of the British Aircraft Corporation (now British Aerospace)/ Aérospacial *Concorde* landing after a test flight. The steamlined nose section of the aeroplane is tilted down on landing to allow the pilot a clearer view of the runway.

The *Tu-144* uses four Kuznetsov NK-144 afterburning turbofans each with a thrust of 180,000 kg (396,825 lb).

A wingspan of 28.8 m (94.5 ft) and a length of 65.7 m (215.5 ft) make the *Tu-144* slightly larger than *Concorde*. Top speed is Mach 2.35, slightly faster than *Concorde*.

A disastrous crash while on demonstration at the Paris Air Show in 1973 delayed further development. It was in passenger service from 1977 to 1978 between Moscow and Alma Alta. Because of technical and fuel problems it was then withdrawn from service.

Any future design for a supersonic aircraft will have to carry a much larger number of passengers to be economical. To achieve higher speeds new materials will have to be developed for the skin of the aircraft.

While passenger transport is still the major part of the commercial airlines' business, there is an increasing amount of cargo carried by air. The military particularly have a need to ship both men and machinery rapidly to any point of the world. Special large air transporters have been developed to carry particularly large or awkward cargoes.

LOCKHEED C-5B GALAXY

The largest aircraft flying today is the massive Lockheed C-5B *Galaxy* which is used by the USAF as a heavy strategic transporter. As part of a 'rapid deployment force' it is designed to carry both men and machines as quickly as possible to any part of the world where army support is required.

Developed from the C-5A *Galaxy* which was first produced in 1973, the C-5B is powered by four 18,643 kg (41,100 lb) thrust General

Above and right: The Super Guppy is an air transporter which was developed from an existing aircraft.

Electric TF39-GE-1C turbofans. It is 75.53 m (247 ft 10 in) in length with a wing span of 67.88 m (222 ft 8 in). The *Galaxy* is 19.34 m (65 ft 1½ in) high. With its maximum payload of 179,177 kg (422,000 lb) the *Galaxy* has a range of 4390 km (2728 miles). The aeroplane carries a crew of five and has 15 passenger seats on the flight deck, 75 seats in an aft troop compartment and up to 270 troop seats on pallets in the cargo compartment. Up to 36 standard cargo pallets or a number of military vehicles can be carried.

The maximum speed of the *Galaxy* is 919 km/h (571 mph) at a height of 7620 m (25,000 ft).

The *Galaxy* transporter fleet is supported by earlier Lockheed C-130 *Hercules* turboprop transporters and modified *DC-10* and *Tristar* airliners.

A new transporter, the McDonnell-Douglas C-17 is planned to replace the *Hercules* in the 1990s. With a heavier and larger payload the C-17 would also have the advantage of being able to take-off and land on restricted length runways which have been quickly prepared.

A new large transporter code-named the CX-C is under development as an eventual replacement for the *Galaxy*. This aeroplane will be even larger than the *Galaxy* but more able to land on ill-prepared landing strips.

SUPER GUPPY

The most ungainly-looking air transporter in use today is the turbo-prop powered Super Guppy 201 which is used to ferry A300 *Airbus* subassemblies (such as wings) to the final assembly plant at Toulouse, France. The name comes from its likeness in appearance to a particular freshwater fish.

The *Super Guppy* is converted from a Boeing *377* airliner. It has a wing span of 47.62 m (156 ft 3 in) and a length of 43.84 m (143 ft 10 in). Four Allinson 501-D22C turboprop engines power the aeroplane at a maximum speed of 463 km/h

Left: Loading military vehicles on to a Lockheed Galaxy air transporter, the world's largest aircraft. The cargo bay is 40 m (131.2 ft) long and 6 m (19.68 ft) wide. Loading is made easy by the use of a large hinged nose on the aircraft.

Below: Two British short-range *Lightning* intercept fighters refuelling from a *Victor* tanker. A drogue can be seen clearly at the nose of the fighter on the left. Long distance air transporter movements depend on efficient tanker refuelling operations to extend their range and payload.

(288 mph). The *Super Guppy* has a maximum cargo capacity of 24,494 kg (53,000 lb) but a range of only 813 km (505 miles).

REFUELLING IN FLIGHT

To allow military aeroplanes to travel over greater distances without refuelling, fuel tanker converted aeroplanes are used. Based on commercial airliners or on military transporters the tankers use a system of booms or drogues to pass fuel to specially equipped fighter, bomber or transporter aeroplanes.

The British system uses a drogue (a cone shaped object which is supported by wind pressure) valve connection trailed on the end of a flexible pipe to mate with a hollow probe mounted at the front of the refuelling aircraft.

The American system uses a telescopic boom with a winged tip which can be directed by an operator on the tanker to inject fuel directly into the tank of the following aircraft.

To achieve extreme range at maximum payload, fighters and attack aircraft sometimes refuel three times in the course of a mission, and the tankers themselves are topped up by other tankers.

Above: The *Nimrod* is a sophisticated early warning and detection aircraft, designed to replace the ageing *Shackleton*.

The balance of weapons between the major world powers is a fine one. Part of this balance depends on the ability to detect an enemy missile attack as early as possible and direct defence and countermeasures in response. Traditionally this has been done by sensitive ground-based radar systems. However, these systems are limited in their detection range by the shielding effect of the curvature of the Earth's surface.

One solution to this particular problem is to take the radar up into the air on board special aircraft. The RAF's *Nimrod AEW* (Advanced Early Warning) and the USAF's *AWACS* (Advanced Warning and Control System) aircraft are two sophisticated examples of this type of machine.

NIMROD

The British Aerospace *Nimrod* AEW Mark 3 is a highly-advanced radar carrying detection aircraft.

The aircraft has a wingspan of 35.08 (115 ft) and a length of 41.97 m (137.6 ft). It is powered by four Rolls Royce RB 168-20 Spey Mark 250 turbofans. Take-off weight is 85,185 kg (190,000 lb) and the aircraft has a maximum endurance time of over ten hours. The *Nimrod* is designed to stay on station for at least seven hours at a height of 10,670 m (35,000 ft) at up to 1600 km (1000 miles) from base.

The crew of the *Nimrod* consists of four flight crew, a tactical air control officer, an 'Electronic Warfare Support Systems' operator and three air direction operators.

To help detect enemy submarines the *Nimrod* carries a number of sonar buoys which can be dropped by parachute to help locate the highly elusive submerged vessels. Sonar buoys operate by sending out and then analysing sound waves reflected back by underwater objects. Submarines have characteristic sound 'signatures' and their distance, depth and direction can be calculated from signals transmitted back to the aircraft by the buoys.

The main radar equipment of the *Nimrod* consists of two identical radar scanners situated in two large bulbous protrusions to the front and rear of the aircraft. These 180° radar scanners are synchronized to give a continuous sweep through 360°.

A particular advantage of this type of radar is its ability to detect low-flying aircraft or missiles that would normally be below the horizon of ground-based radar.

The aircraft also has weather radar systems located in pods below the wings. Electronic Warfare pods at the wing tips are designed to confuse enemy radar and guidance systems.

The radar equipment on this aircraft is very sophisticated and problems have delayed the start of operational duties for the *Nimrod*.

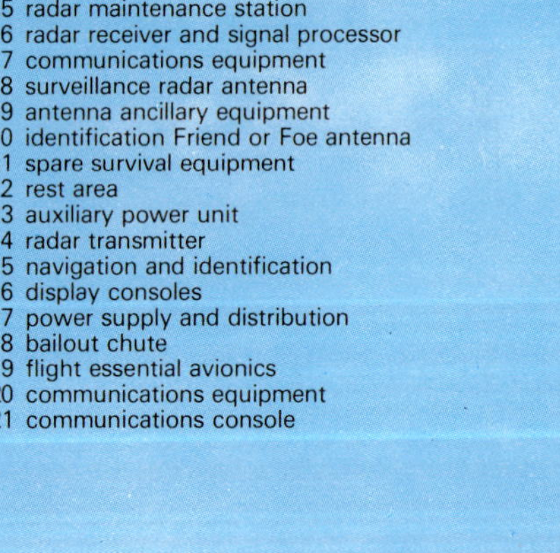

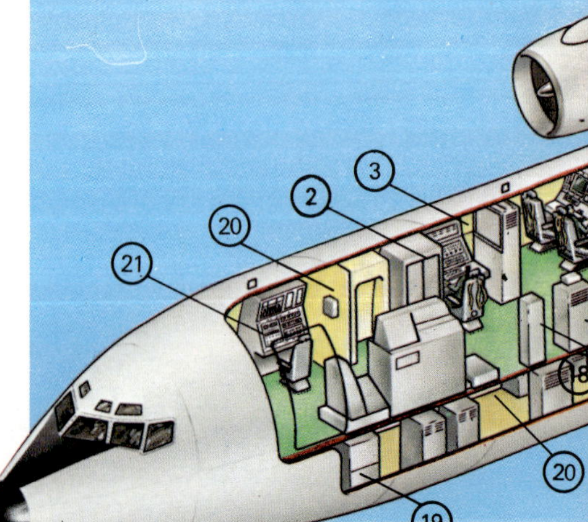

THE SENTRY E-3

The Boeing E-3 *Sentry* is the American equivalent of *Nimrod*. It has a wingspan of 44.92 m (145.75 ft). Powered by four Pratt & Whitney TF33-PW-100A turbofans, it has a maximum time on station of six hours cruising at 605 km/h (376 mph) without refuelling. The maximum take-off weight is 147,420 kg (325,000 lb).

The *Sentry* uses a flight crew of four and operational crew of 13. The operational crew consists of a battle commander, a team of eight air defence crew and a maintenance crew of four.

Like the Russian Ilyushin *Mainstay* early warning aircraft, but unlike *Nimrod*, the *Sentry* uses a large rotating radar scanner (radome) mounted above the aircraft. This produces a radar blind spot below the aircraft.

The first prototype aircraft flew in 1972 and a number are now in full operational service. At least one *Sentry* is on station at all times.

Left: Only when a submarine surfaces is it easily detected.

Below: A Boeing E-3 *Sentry* is an integrated surveillance command and control system. The 9 m (29.5 ft) diameter radome has a range of up to 400 km (285 miles).

THE SEA KING

Experience in the Falklands War, where the main difficulty experienced by the British fleet was in detecting enemy attack early enough, has led to the development of helicopter based early warning systems.

Eight Westland *Sea King* helicopters have been equipped with Thorn-EMI searchwater radar systems. The radar scanners are mounted in an inflatable weatherproof bag which is positioned below the helicopter in flight.

Stationed above the fleet the helicopter can give much earlier warning of low level enemy attack. The *Sea King* also provides invaluable anti-submarine warfare systems and a search and rescue capability.

One of the most remarkable aircraft ever built is the Hawker-Siddeley *Harrier* VSTOL (Vertical or Short Take-Off and Landing) fighter aircraft.

THE FLYING BEDSTEAD

Research on vertical take-off and landing aircraft began in Britain in 1953 with the construction of the *Flying Bedstead* test rig.

The *Flying Bedstead* (so called because of its resemblance to a bedstead with four long castor wheeled legs and an open metal framework) was a rig built by Rolls-Royce to test the practicality of building vertical take-off aircraft. Powered by two *Nene* engines, and stabilized by compressed air nozzles mounted on outrigger arms, the *Flying Bedstead* provided much invaluable research information.

The rig weighed 3250 kg (7200 lb) and the two engines gave a thrust of 3600 kg (8000 lb).

THE P1127

In 1961 Hawker-Siddeley first flew their experimental *P1127*.

The *P1127* was powered by a single Rolls-Royce Bristol Pegasus jet engine which provided power through four 'vectored thrust' ducts which could swivel to provide vertical or horizontal thrust. Like the *Flying Bedstead* the aircraft was stabilized by four gas jets which were mounted at the nose and tail and on the wing tips. These assisted particularly at the point of transition from vertical to horizontal flight.

The *P1127* demonstrated an ability to take-off vertically, hover, go forwards, backwards or even sideways.

It was some years later that the *P1127* became the highly successful *Harrier* jet fighter.

THE HARRIER

The *Harrier* became operational in 1969. It had one major advantage over any other fixed wing fighter—it did not need an airstrip to take-off or land on. It could be hidden in a clearing in a forest and provide

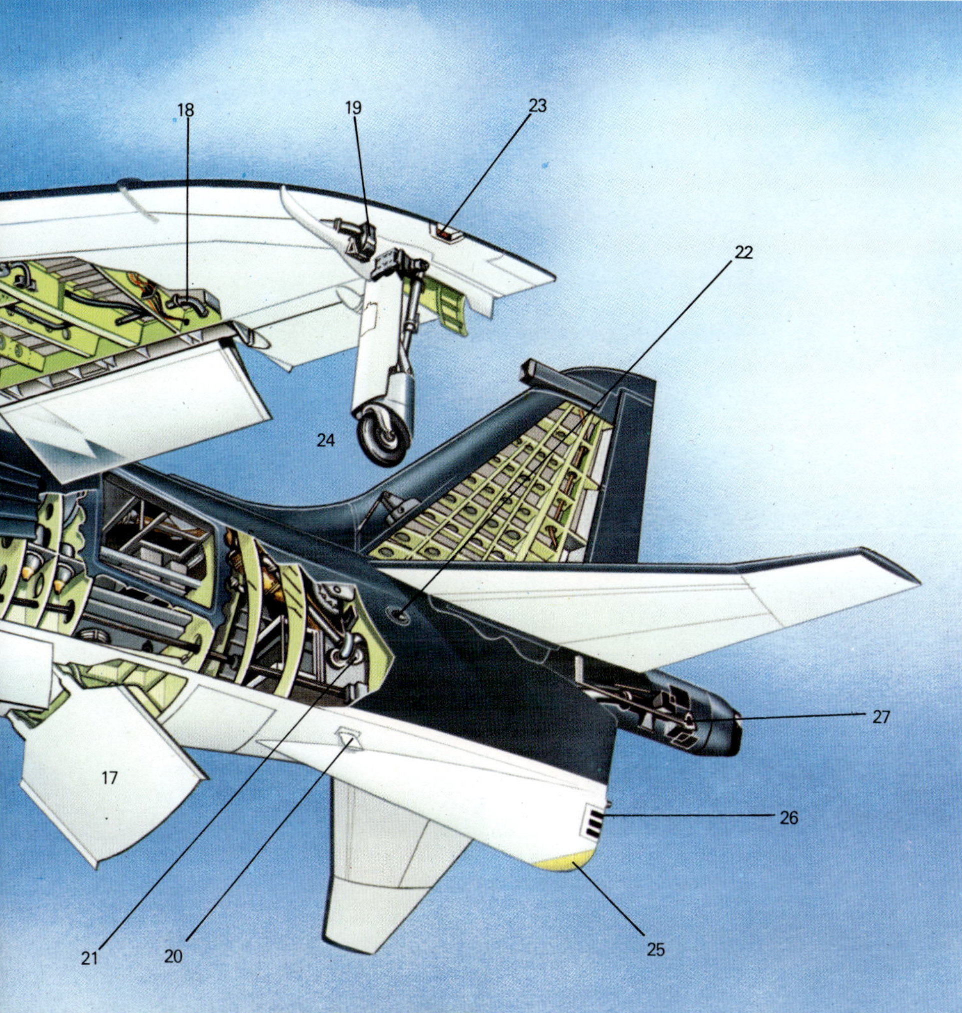

1 pilot probe
2 detachable nose cone
3 duct to pitch reaction nozzle
4 landing lamp
5 steering motor
6 first stage fan
7 Pegasus 102 turbofan engine
8 port front tank
9 refuelling probe light
10 starboard 30mm Aden gun
11 fuel drop tank
12 sidewinder air-to-air missile
13 nozzles
14 gear box
15 ground refuelling point
16 duct pitch and yaw reaction nozzle
17 airbrake
18 jettison valve
19 roll control system
20 UHF aerial
21 turbine exhaust
22 ram air exhaust
23 navigation light
24 rudder linkage
25 glass fibre bumper
26 IFF notch aerial
27 yaw/pitch control valves

Below left: The McDonnell Douglas AV-8B which is in service with the US Marine Corps. It makes extensive use of carbon fibre construction to reduce weight and increase payload.

limited the aircraft's weapon carrying capacity. To help increase this payload, short take-off runs were used and a 'ski-slope' raked platform was introduced to assist more heavily laden take-offs.

Short take-off and landing techniques have also meant the development of smaller and less expensive aircraft carriers.

THE AV-8B

The most advanced version of the *Harrier* in service is the *AV-8B* which was first flown in 1981.

The *AV-8B* is built under licence in America by McDonnell Douglas. Extensive use of carbon fibre laminates in the wing and fuselage of the aircraft have resulted in a significant saving in weight. Improved vector nozzles and wing

shape have increased lift. An extended tail is fitted and the cockpit is raised.

The single Rolls-Royce F402-RR-406 Pegasus turbofan engine produces a thrust of 9775 kg (21,550 lb). The maximum speed in forwards flight is 1075 km/h (688 mph).

The wing span is 9.24 m (30.3 ft) and the length of the fuselage is 14.12 m (46.3 ft).

The empty weight of the aircraft is 5783 kg (12,750 lb). For vertical take-off the maximum weight is 8702 kg (19,185 lb) and for short take-off 13,495 kg (29,750 lb). The payload or radius of operations are twice that of the original *Harrier*.

One 25 mm five-barrel rotary cannon is fitted and up to 4173 kg (9200 lb) of ordnance can be carried.

The *Harrier* has proved a very successful combat aircraft with 'vectored thrust' techniques giving increased manoeuvrability over conventional aircraft.

Work is underway on the development of supersonic versions of the *Harrier*.

rapid air cover for troops.

The main disadvantage of the aircraft was that vertical take-off used up a large amount of fuel and

THE HELICOPTER

The most versatile aircraft type today is the helicopter. Helicopters use a number of horizontally rotating aerofoil blades to provide lift. Unlike fixed wing aircraft (apart from VSTOL aircraft) which depend on forwards speed for lift, they are able to take-off vertically, hover, change direction and land on any small relatively flat area.

For military support and strike, cargo carrying, support transport for oil rigs, passenger transport to city centres and air-sea rescue operations they have few real rivals.

Many different shapes and sizes of helicopter have been produced for both civil and military uses with single and multiple rotor designs.

Large twin rotor helicopters are often used to perform heavy lifting operations, performing as aerial cranes. The two rotors may be mounted for and aft of the main fuselage or at the sides.

The standard single rotor helicopter needs a second smaller rotor mounted vertically on a long boom to counteract the spinning effect that is imparted by the rotating main blades. This results in the shape of helicopter that we see most often. Recently research into the use of jet thrust nozzles to replace this second rotor has been undertaken and a number of experimental craft built.

BELL 214ST

This is a typical modern single main rotor helicopter. Although

Above: The vast bulk of the Boeing CH-47C Chinook. This helicopter is capable of carrying heavy loads. It is used both for civil and military purposes, and is seen here at Farnborough.

it is not revolutionary in design it incorporates a number of interesting design features.

The Bell *214 Super Transport* is powered by two General Electric CT7-2A turboshaft engines each with a power of 1210 kw (1625 hp). The rotor diameter is 15.88 m (52 ft) and the fuselage is 15.24 m (50 ft) long.

The *214ST* has a maximum cruising speed of 264 km/h (164 mph) and a maximum hovering height of 3840 m (12,600 ft).

Eighteen passengers and two crew can travel up to 740 km (460 miles). The maximum take-off weight (with either an internal or external load) is 7938 kg (17,500 lb).

The two large rotor blades, almost a metre (3.25 ft) wide, are made of glass fibre and plastic laminate which is tipped with stainless steel and edged with titanium for protection against damage and abrasion.

The rotor is attached to the main body of the helicopter via a special 'nodal' suspension system which helps eliminate vibration.

An onboard computer permanently monitors the condition of the engines, eliminating most routine maintenance and providing a continuous check on performance.

Another computer system maintains the correct flying altitude —automatically ensuring maximum efficiency, and also trims the rotor pitch for maximum lift.

External conditions including

Fact file . . .

The world's largest helicopter is the Russian Mil-12 *Homer* which weighs over 100 tonnes and can lift a payload of over 39.5 tonnes. A payload of 56.77 tonnes has been lifted by a Russian Mil-26 helicopter. The Aerospace General Co's one-man rocket assisted minicopter weighs only 72.5 kg (160 lb).

Above: As an oil rig support vehicle the Bell 214ST is capable of carrying up to 18 passengers and operating in bad weather over water.
Military transport versions of this helicopter have also been produced.

temperature and pressure are constantly monitored and the economical flying height and speed calculated.

A further system called SCAS (Stability and Control Augmentation System) acts to damp out small movements in pitch, roll and yaw as the helicopter hits air turbulence.

The AARS (Attitude/Altitude Retention System) allows hands-off cruising for long flights. It can be set to fly the helicopter forwards, sideways or backwards.

The Bell *214ST* is one of the first helicopters to meet safety regulations allowing it to fly passengers over water in all weather conditions. This makes this helicopter ideal for servicing offshore oil drilling rigs.

Above: A Westland *Sea King* helicopter on submarine detection patrol with the Royal Navy. It is in the process of retrieving a sonar probe.

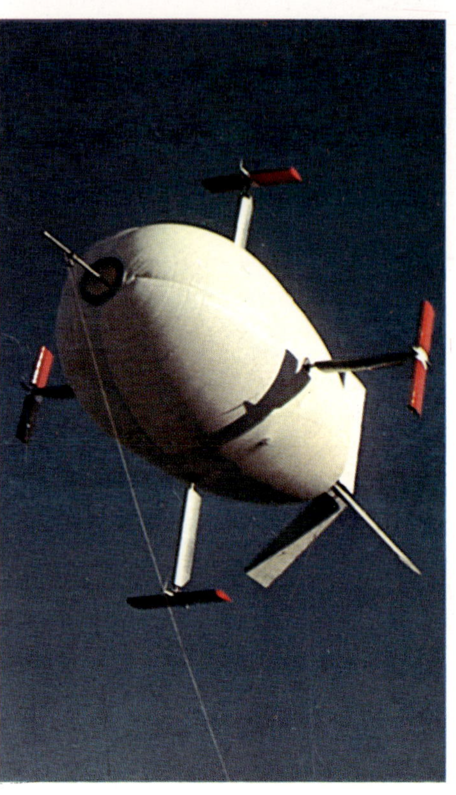

Above: The Cyclo-Crane offers increased lifting powers and control as a possible rival for the cargo-carrying helicopter.

Left: A once familiar sight returns to the skies. Here, the Airship Industries Skyship 500 visits a North Sea oil rig. Soon it is hoped that much larger passenger and cargo airships will come into service.

Three years before the historic first aeroplane flight by the Wright brothers, the first flight of a German airship took place. The airship was built by Count Ferdinand von Zeppelin who went on to form the world's first passenger airline. Over 10,000 passengers were carried before the outbreak of World War I. The Germans were not allowed to build any more airships until 1928 when the LZ127 *Graf Zeppelin* was named in honour of the Count.

The *Graf Zeppelin* was over 235 metres (770 ft) long and weighed 117 tonnes. It had a crew of forty and carried twenty passengers. The airship had a rigid aluminium framework covered with a fabric skin. Gasbags mounted inside the framework carried 104,700 cubic metres (3,700,000 cubic feet) of hydrogen gas.

Graf Zeppelin made its first Atlantic crossing in 1928 and a circumnavigation of the world in 1929. Before it was retired in 1937 the *Graf Zeppelin* had travelled over 1,610,000 km (1,000,000 miles) and carried over 13,000 passengers without incident.

The even larger German airship the *Hindenburg*, weighing over 200 tonnes and carrying 50 passengers, suffered a disastrous accident in 1937 when approaching Lakehurst in the USA. The *Hindenburg* burst into flames and thirty-six people were killed. A number of other

Above: In the large hanger that housed giant pre-war airships a circular rig is being used to test and improve the ground handling of airships.

accidents to airships, and fears about the highly flammable nature of the hydrogen lifting gas, signalled the end of the airship's domination of the skies.

The increasing cost of fuel and the availability of a safe lifting gas, helium, led eventually to the reconsideration of the airship as a practical means of transport.

The Airship Industries *Skyship 500* is a typical modern airship. Built in a corner of the enormous hanger that had housed the giant British *R101* airship before World War II, the *Skyship 500* is, like most modern airships, a non-rigid structure made from polyester and filled with helium gas. The gondola, or cabin, is made from a strong plastic material called Kevlar. The tailfin and bulkheads are made from a 'honey comb' material similar to that used on high speed boats.

As no power is required to lift the airship, which is lighter than air, the engines can be quite small and the *Skyship 500* uses two *Porche 930* six cylinder car engines which drive five bladed fans on either side of the gondola. The fans can be rotated to provide vectored thrust upwards, downwards or forwards, and give a maximum speed of 115 km/h (62 knots).

The *Skyship 500* is 50 metres (164 ft), long, only a fraction of the size of earlier airships. Long term plans include the construction of airships to carry up to 200 passengers. Airships like the *Skyship 500* are used for advertising and coastal patrol.

Several countries, including Russia and Canada, are working to develop cargo-carrying airships.

In the USA, Aerolift Inc. has been developing the *Cyclo-Crane* which increases the lift it can provide by the use of rotating airfoils.

The weight of the structure of the *Cyclo-Crane* and half the weight of the cargo are supported by the aerostatic lift due to lighter-than-air helium gas contained in the balloon envelope. The rest of the lift and thrust comes from a system of airfoils that rotate, when the *Cyclo-Crane* is hovering, and move to become aligned with the direction of flight when the *Cyclo-Crane* reaches its maximum forward speed. The *Cyclo-Crane* is designed to rotate at 16 rpm when hovering but slows down to compensate for increased lift from the airfoils in forward flight.

The *Cyclo-Crane* is designed to be as easy to operate as a helicopter and to offer much lower capital and operational costs. Interest has been expressed in the use of the *Cyclo-Crane* by Canadian forestry workers who see its potential for transporting felled trees from inaccessible areas. A 50 tonne *Cyclo-Crane* could carry about 550 passengers in a transport 'pod' which would be slung beneath the craft.

A rotating balloon is also envisaged in a design by the Canadian Van Dusen Company. This airship design is a 54.9 m (195 ft) diameter sphere which rotates about a horizontal axis. The 'Magnus effect' of the rotation of the sphere in the direction of flight gives increased and controllable lift. A yoke, suspended from the axis of rotation, contains the cockpit and cargo area which is designed to have a capacity of about 60,000 kg (132,240 lb).

Fact file . . .

The first flight of a powered airship took place on 24 September 1852. Built by Henri Giffard, this steam powered, coal gas filled airship flew 27 km (17 miles) at a speed of 8 km/h (5 mph).

The US Navy Akron airship carried the largest ever passenger load of 207 in 1931.

NEW SKY SHAPES

The shapes of aircraft constantly change as new engines and new materials are developed. Higher technology allows much more adventurous designs to be built and the search for increased efficiency smooths and shapes the contours of the aircraft. Small business aircraft have become more important and the traditional, conservative, designs are giving way to more exciting and fanciful aircraft types.

Military aircraft designs change most rapidly as governments try to gain superiority in the air by stretching technology to its limits.

The *Learfan 2100* is a small business passenger aircraft that has used new materials to increase efficiency and performance. The aircraft is constructed extensively of carbon fibre laminates which have a much improved strength-to-weight ratio over traditional metal construction techniques. In fact the only metal parts of the structure are the undercarriage and the engines. Bulkheads, control surfaces and propeller blades are made of Kevlar reinforced plastic.

A pusher propeller is used and this is powered by two turboshaft engines. The propeller is driven via two clutches and a reduction gearbox. The aircraft is streamlined and results with a prototype aircraft show a 25% increase in performance with a 50% reduction in fuel use over its more conventional rivals. Unfortunately, financial and political problems may prevent this highly original design from coming into service.

The *Edgeley EA7 Optica* was designed in the UK as an observation aircraft. It is a very efficient and unusual design which can provide a similar service to observation helicopters at a much lower operating cost.

A wide view cockpit is mounted in front of a ducted fan engine. The aircraft is designed to cruise at low speeds with a long flight duration. It is ideal for use in traffic surveillance, aerial photography, frontier patrol and similar jobs.

The aircraft uses a single Avco Lycoming IO-540 six-cylinder, horizontally-opposed engine, which provides 194 kw (260 hp) of power to a fixed pitch five-bladed fan.

Maximum speed is 213 km/h (156 mph) with a loitering speed of

Above Right: A Boeing concept of the JVX tilt-rotor military transport vehicle which is designed to incorporate the best of both helicopters and conventional aircraft.

Right: The highly original design of the Learfan 2100 gives much increased fuel efficiency.

98 km/h (61 mph). The aircraft has a maximum duration at loitering speed of 6.5 hours and a range of 869 km (540 miles).

Wingspan is 12 metres (39.3 ft), and the length 8.15 metres (26.75 ft). The empty weight is 850 kg (1875 lb) and maximum take-off weight is 1236 kg (2725 lb). The *Optica* can take off in only 300 metres (980 ft) and land in 250 metres (820 ft).

Costing less than a third of the operating costs of a helicopter, the *Optica* has proved very popular with many countries since it went into production in 1985.

Military bodies can demand large budgets for experimental research into weapons technology. It is not, therefore, surprising that the most advanced aircraft flying today are military ones.

Designs for ever faster and more manoeuvrable fighter aircraft have resulted in the *HiMAT* (Highly Manoeuvrable Aircraft Technology) concept. This concept uses canards (forward mounted

Far left: The Rockwell HiMAT research aircraft type demonstrates its high manoeuvrability as an intercept fighter.

Below: The Edgeley Optica is an ideal light aircraft for slow speed observation work being much more economical than the helicopter it can replace.

winglets) and a blended wing/body shape with tip fins and dual rudders. Weighing just 11 tonnes, a *HiMAT* fighter would be capable of sustained 8 g (8 times the force of gravity) turns.

Aeroelastic construction would allow wings and canards to bend and flex. Computers would be used to constantly twist and adjust the control surfaces of the aircraft to stabilize the flight. Much of the aircraft would be built of plastics and composite materials.

Future offensive aircraft are being built with the concept of Stealth. Stealth is a design objective which aims at the aircraft being as difficult to detect as possible by enemy radar and other detection systems.

The use of composite materials and careful design of the aircraft's shape can reduce its reflected image on a radar screen. Radar absorbent plastics and paints are being developed. All vertical surfaces are reduced or eliminated. Corners are blended into gentle curves. Ultimately the aircraft may become just a flying wing.

Engines are hidden behind baffles to protect them from radar detection and exhaust shields reduce the possibility of the aircraft being detected by heat sensors. Noise absorbing material will also be incorporated.

Computer control of the aircraft allows fins and rudders to be reduced in size or even eliminated. Their own radar systems will become lower powered and more sophisticated.

The Stealthy aircraft will never become completely invisible but its detection will become much more difficult. Troop and cargo transporters will also develop; the latest concept is that of the *JVX* tilt-rotor transport which is a combination of the versatility of helicopters and the speed, and efficiency of conventional aircraft.

Rotors are mounted horizontally for a vertical take-off but in flight rotate forwards to become conventional propellers.

SPACE

In the 20th century the one remaining frontier to conquer was space. Tremendous power would be required to overcome the gravitational pull of the Earth. It was only with the development of rocket engines burning highly explosive fuel that this became possible.

Man has only just begun his exploration of space and the Super-machines he has used are only the prototypes of yet more amazing rockets and spaceships to come. The next steps in space exploration will include large orbiting space factories and manned space missions to other planets of the solar system.

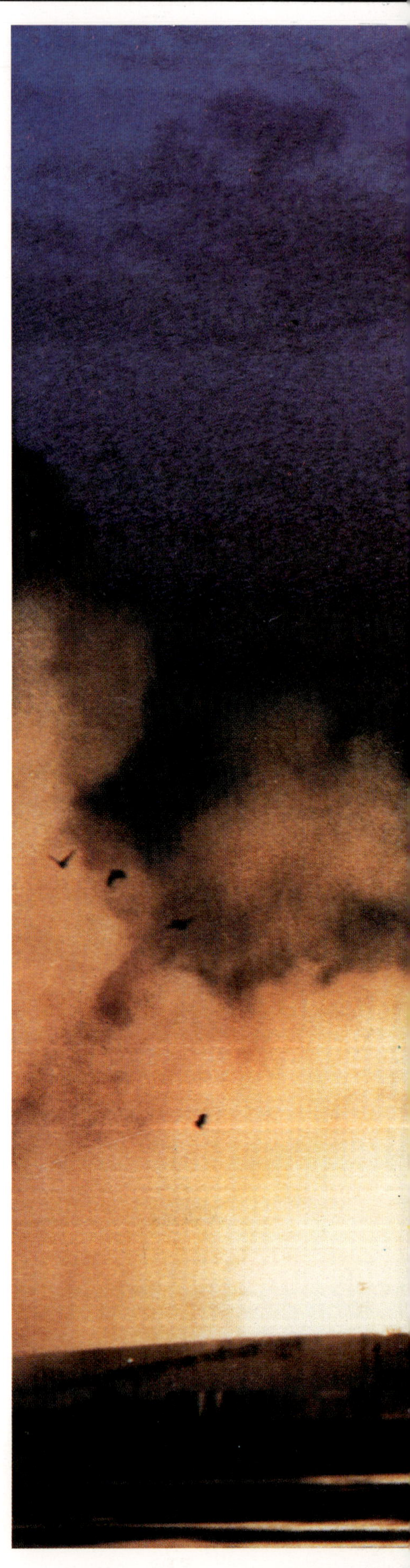

The Saturn V rocket which launched the North American Space Administration (NASA)'s Apollo manned Moon landing missions was the largest rocket ever launched.

THE SHUTTLE

Having achieved its primary mission of a manned landing on the Moon, NASA (the North American Space Administration) began to look into the possibilities of reducing the immense costs involved in the use of one-off rockets and capsules.

The Space Shuttle project was conceived as a way of reducing these costs by making much of the space vehicle and its equipment recoverable and reusable.

This process involved the development of new and advanced technologies. The Shuttle was designed to carry large and varied payloads, to be a launch platform for satellites, and to carry advanced experimental laboratories for various scientific projects. At the end of the spaceflight the Shuttle returns to Earth with a final gliding descent to an airstrip landing using its aeroplane-like wings.

Work on the Shuttle began in 1972. A prototype Shuttle orbiter, the *Enterprise*, was built in 1977 and this completed a number of trial landings and other aerodynamic tests.

The first operational Shuttle orbiter *Columbia* was due to fly in 1979 but problems with heat shields and engines delayed this until 12 April 1981.

The immense heat of re-entry into the Earth's atmosphere (over 1500°C), caused by friction with the molecules of the air at high speeds, would be enough to melt most metals and alloys.

To solve this problem the Shuttle's surface is covered with over 30,000 special ceramic tiles which insulate the metal skin of the fuselage.

One of the many payloads that have been carried in the 18 metres (60 ft) long by 4.5 metres (15 ft) diameter payload bay of the Space Shuttle is Spacelab. This device allows

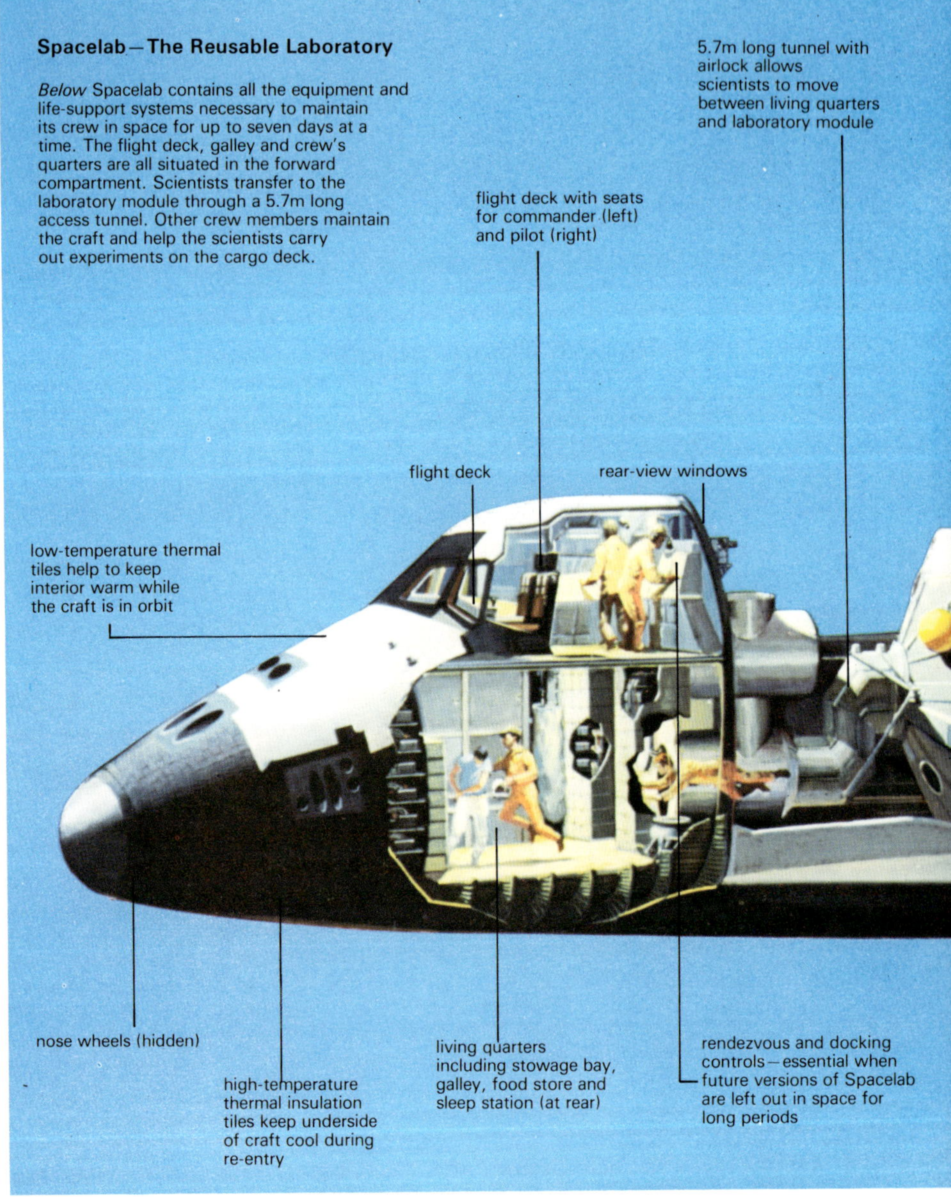

Below Spacelab contains all the equipment and life-support systems necessary to maintain its crew in space for up to seven days at a time. The flight deck, galley and crew's quarters are all situated in the forward compartment. Scientists transfer to the laboratory module through a 5.7m long access tunnel. Other crew members maintain the craft and help the scientists carry out experiments on the cargo deck.

scientists to work in a zero gravity, high vacuum environment on the development of new engineering, scientific and medical processes.

It is expected that new alloys and more effective drugs can be developed and manufactured under these conditions.

The Spacelab also assists with research into the longterm development of permanent large space stations.

To counter the gravitational pull of the Earth and attain orbit the Shuttle still requires the immense power of rockets. These rockets use large amounts of highly dangerous fuel either in liquid or solid form.

The Shuttle uses an external liquid fuel tank which feeds its own engines, and also two solid fuel boosters which are designed to separate about two minutes after launch and are later recovered after returning to Earth on parachutes. The liquid fuel tank, which contains separate tanks of liquid hydrogen and liquid oxygen cooled to low temperatures, continues to power the Shuttle's engines for about six minutes. The tank then separates from the Shuttle orbiter and breaks up as it re-enters the Earth's atmosphere.

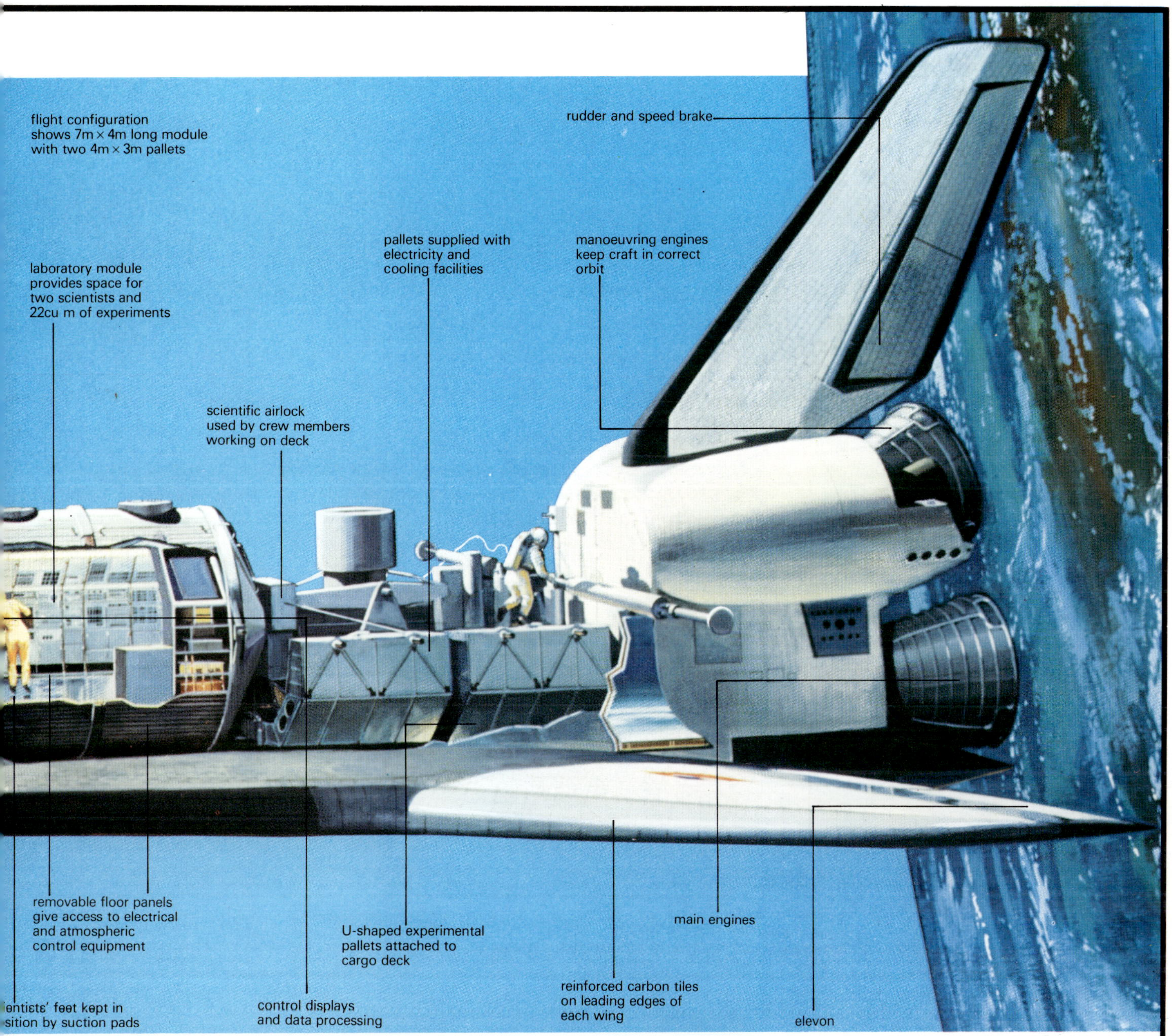

flight configuration
shows 7m × 4m long module
with two 4m × 3m pallets

rudder and speed brake

laboratory module
provides space for
two scientists and
22cu m of experiments

pallets supplied with
electricity and
cooling facilities

manoeuvring engines
keep craft in correct
orbit

scientific airlock
used by crew members
working on deck

removable floor panels
give access to electrical
and atmospheric
control equipment

U-shaped experimental
pallets attached to
cargo deck

main engines

scientists' feet kept in
position by suction pads

control displays
and data processing

reinforced carbon tiles
on leading edges of
each wing

elevon

Left: The Shuttle seen moments after lift-off. The liquid fuel tank and the two solid fuel boosters can be seen clearly as can the immense power produced by the rocket engines to lift the Shuttle orbiter into space. The fuel of the solid fuel rockets is used up within two minutes.

Two manoeuvring engines on the Shuttle then place it in orbit about 250 kilometres (150 miles) high.

A tragic accident on 28 January 1986 only 74 seconds into the flight emphasized the dangerous nature of spaceflight. The crew of seven died in an explosion.

SALYUT

The USSR launched the world's first artificial satellite *Sputnik 1* in 1957. This was followed by the first manned spaceflight in 1961 when Yuri Gagarin became the first cosmonaut in the *Vostok 1* space capsule.

The USA then became determined to put the first men on the Moon. They achieved this when Neil Armstrong and William (Buzz) Aldrin landed their *Apollo 11* mission on the Moon's surface on 20 July 1969. After a number of Moon missions and the development of *Skylab* (a space station which was occupied for 84 days in 1974) the *Apollo/Saturn 5* rocket programme was abandoned. The American space programme then concentrated on the development of the Shuttle.

The Soviet space programme also changed direction as it abandoned its own manned Moon landing programme in favour of unmanned exploration, and started a long term project based on standard rocket launchers and space capsules. Their first space station *Salyut 1* was launched in April 1971.

SALYUT 1

Salyut 1 weighed nearly 20 tonnes and was 22 metres (71.5 ft) long and 4 metres (13 ft) in diameter. It obtained its operational power from solar cells which folded out once the station was in orbit.

The space station was placed in orbit by an unmanned launcher rocket. The first occupation of the station occurred in June 1971 when cosmonauts Georgi Dobrovolski, Vladislav Volkov and Victor Patsayev docked their capsule *Soyuz 11*. They remained on board for more than three weeks. On transferring back to their capsule a pressure valve burst open and all three men died.

The next space station *Salyut 2* was unmanned and sent back information automatically.

The launch of *Salyut 3* brought the return of manned operation with an occupation of 16 days in July 1974. Two sets of cosmonauts occupied *Salyut 4* which was launched in December 1974, the second visit lasting for 62 days. *Salyut 5* received two more cosmonaut teams before the launch of *Salyut 6* on 29 September 1977.

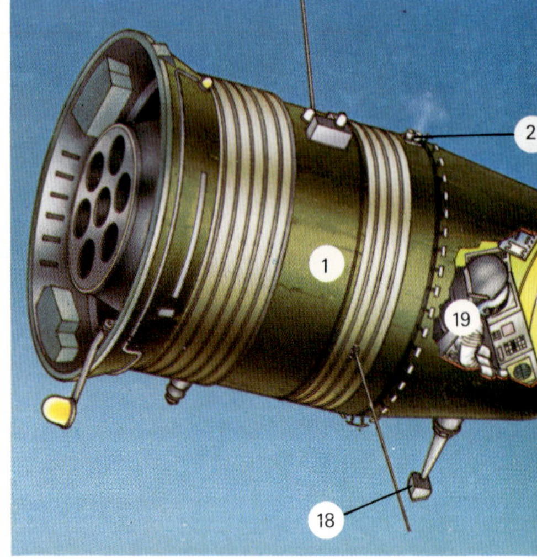

SALYUT 6

After an abortive first attempt to deliver a crew to *Salyut 6* Yuri Romanenko and Georgi Grechko occupied the station for 96 days from 10 December 1977. During this time Romanenko and Grechko were visited by a Czech pilot Vladimir Remek who stayed for eight days and also by a *Progress* unmanned spacecraft ferrying fuel and cargo to the space station.

Three months after this flight was completed a team of cosmonauts occupied *Salyut 6* for 140 days with several visits from other cosmonauts. The next flight, which began on 25 February 1979, kept cosmonauts Lyakhov and Ryumin in orbit for nearly six months—but this time with no visitors.

The purpose of these ever longer spaceflights was to test the ability of man to endure long periods in space. If man is to travel on long journeys to the planets this knowledge is vital.

One of the long term goals of the Soviet programme is a manned mission to Mars. This would involve a journey of at least six months in each direction with possibly the need to spend eight months on the planet. To complete the test Valery Ryumin stayed on Earth for eight months and then on 9 April 1980 he returned to *Salyut 6* in the company of Leonid Popov. This time they stayed in orbit for 185 days before returning to Earth.

The results of the *Salyut* experiments show that the human body can cope with this length of space mission. Now further development of the space station and the fabrication of larger vehicles in space will be necessary in order to reach Mars.

The USSR had early successes with its unmanned probes to the Moon. In 1959 *Luna 2* was the first probe to hit the Moon, and *Luna 3* took the first pictures of the hidden far side of the Moon. In 1966 *Luna 9* was the first probe to soft land on the Moon.

Luna 16 brought back samples from the Moon, an achievement that was overshadowed by the earlier American manned landing.

Lunokod 1 was a remarkable robot Moon rover which roamed over the surface of the Moon relaying pictures with its two television cameras and carrying out experiments. It was launched as part of the *Luna 17* probe.

Lunokod 1 travelled at walking pace on its eight wheels. In a 10-month period *Lunokod 1*

Right: The launcher rocket for the Soviet Soyuz space capsules is tiny compared to the Saturn V launcher used by the American Apollo missions. Like most Soviet launch vehicles it uses a number of strap-on booster rockets to assist the first stage.

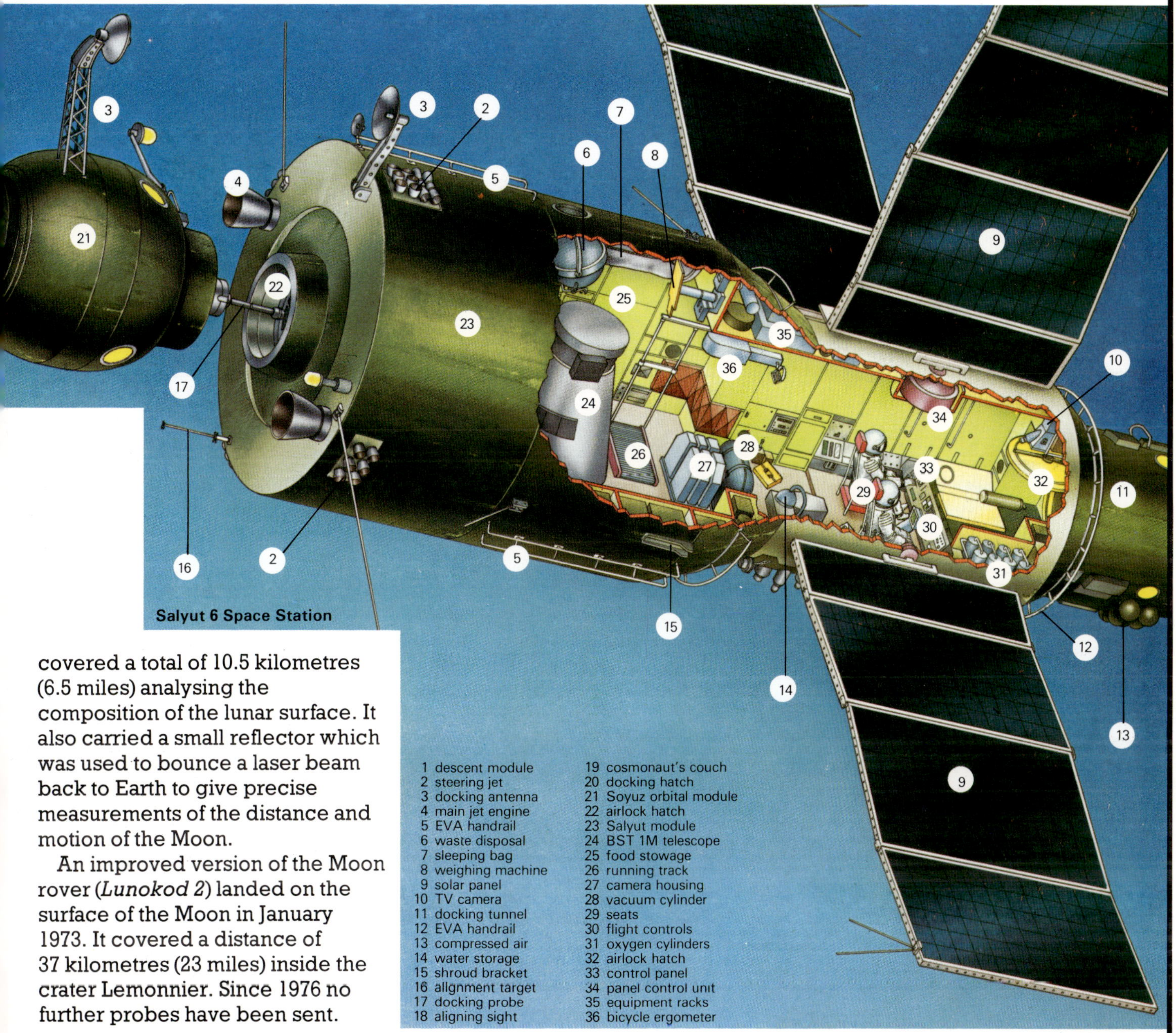

Salyut 6 Space Station

covered a total of 10.5 kilometres (6.5 miles) analysing the composition of the lunar surface. It also carried a small reflector which was used to bounce a laser beam back to Earth to give precise measurements of the distance and motion of the Moon.

An improved version of the Moon rover (*Lunokod 2*) landed on the surface of the Moon in January 1973. It covered a distance of 37 kilometres (23 miles) inside the crater Lemonnier. Since 1976 no further probes have been sent.

1 descent module	19 cosmonaut's couch
2 steering jet	20 docking hatch
3 docking antenna	21 Soyuz orbital module
4 main jet engine	22 airlock hatch
5 EVA handrail	23 Salyut module
6 waste disposal	24 BST 1M telescope
7 sleeping bag	25 food stowage
8 weighing machine	26 running track
9 solar panel	27 camera housing
10 TV camera	28 vacuum cylinder
11 docking tunnel	29 seats
12 EVA handrail	30 flight controls
13 compressed air	31 oxygen cylinders
14 water storage	32 airlock hatch
15 shroud bracket	33 control panel
16 allgnment target	34 panel control unit
17 docking probe	35 equipment racks
18 aligning sight	36 bicycle ergometer

Above: The space probe Lunokod 1 was an eight-wheeled robot probe designed to travel over the Moon.

ROBOT SPACEMEN

Above: The IRAS infra-red space probe on test before being launched by NASA in 1983. The infra-red detectors inside the probe are kept cooled to −270°C by liquid helium.

Manned space probes are used where the special qualities of human observation and reaction are required. For many tasks which involve detailed study over long periods robot probes with remote control from the surface of the Earth are more suitable.

IRAS

A large part of the universe is invisible to observers using visible light. Infra-red light observation is required to reveal low energy sources of radiation such as gas clouds. Certain active galaxies emit large amounts of infra-red radiation, and the centre of our own galaxy is visible by infra-red light shining through surrounding dust clouds. Unfortunately, infra-red observation from the Earth's surface is difficult because of heat variations within the atmosphere.

The *Infra-Red Astronomical Satellite* (IRAS) was launched into an orbit 900 kilometres (643 miles) above the Earth's surface early in 1983. Its task was to make a complete infra-red map of the sky and send this data back to Earth.

This it did with great success and it provided so much data that it will take years to make a full analysis of it. Already, fascinating and useful data has been processed. Almost accidentally *IRAS* helped discover a comet which is now called comet IRAS-Araki-Alcock after its three independent discoverers.

PIONEER

The deep space probe *Pioneer 10* was launched in March 1972 achieving a top speed of 50,000 km/h (31,000 mph) as it sped towards the planet Jupiter. The journey lasted 21 months.

Pioneer 10 passed 130,000 km (81,000 miles) above the clouds of Jupiter, taking exciting pictures as it passed by. A large antenna then transmitted the pictures and other scientific data back to Earth. The success of this probe allowed scientists to redirect the follow-up probe *Pioneer 11*, which had been launched in April 1973, to go much closer to the surface of Jupiter. *Pioneer 11* then continued its journey towards the planet Saturn which it reached and observed some six and a half years after being launched.

Both *Pioneer 10* and *Pioneer 11* are still travelling out of the solar system. Each of them has a gold plaque with a greeting to any space traveller who might find them thousands of years in the future.

VOYAGER

The two *Pioneer* missions were merely pathfinders for the more sophisticated, larger but similar-looking *Voyager* spacecraft. Two *Voyager* probes were launched in late summer 1977. As with *Pioneer* the power for these probes was provided by atomic generators.

The *Voyager* probes looked closely at the moons of Jupiter and then went on to Saturn—*Voyager 1*

Below: An artist's impression of a Pioneer space probe passing close to the cloud-covered surface of Jupiter. The largest part of the probe is the radio antenna which sends information back to Earth.

arriving in November 1980 and *Voyager 2* in August 1981. *Voyager 2* then went on to look at the planet Uranus, arriving there in January 1986. It is now targeted at the planet Neptune which it should reach in September 1989. The results from both probes have surpassed all expectations.

THE SPACE TELESCOPE

The *Space Telescope* was designed to give visible light astronomers the same advantages of atmosphere-free observation that *IRAS* gave to infra-red astronomers. Once launched from the payload bay of the *Shuttle* the *Space Telescope* will be able to make more accurate and detailed observations than any Earth-bound telescope. Scientists expect the telescope to give much better information on little-understood objects like Quasars which may be galaxies in the process of formation.

Fact file . . .

Two NASA *Viking* probes successfully soft landed on the surface of the planet Mars in 1976 and sent back pictures showing a bleak desert landscape.

The probes searched for evidence of life in the soil of Mars but found none.

GIOTTO

Halley's Comet passes close to the sun about every 76 years, a spectacular sight.

On 13 March 1986 the space probe *Giotto* approached the comet as closely as possible to photograph the tiny nucleus and gather data on dust, gases and plasma in the coma and tails of the comet.

Giotto is almost 3 metres (9.84 ft) in height and 1.84 metres (6.03 ft) in diameter. It passed the comet at a speed of approximately 68 km/sec (42.45 miles/sec). *Giotto* was developed by the *European Space Agency* and launched in July 1985 on an *Ariane* rocket launcher. It is one of a number of space probes from various countries that took this rare opportunity to increase our knowledge of the structure of comets and of the universe as a whole.

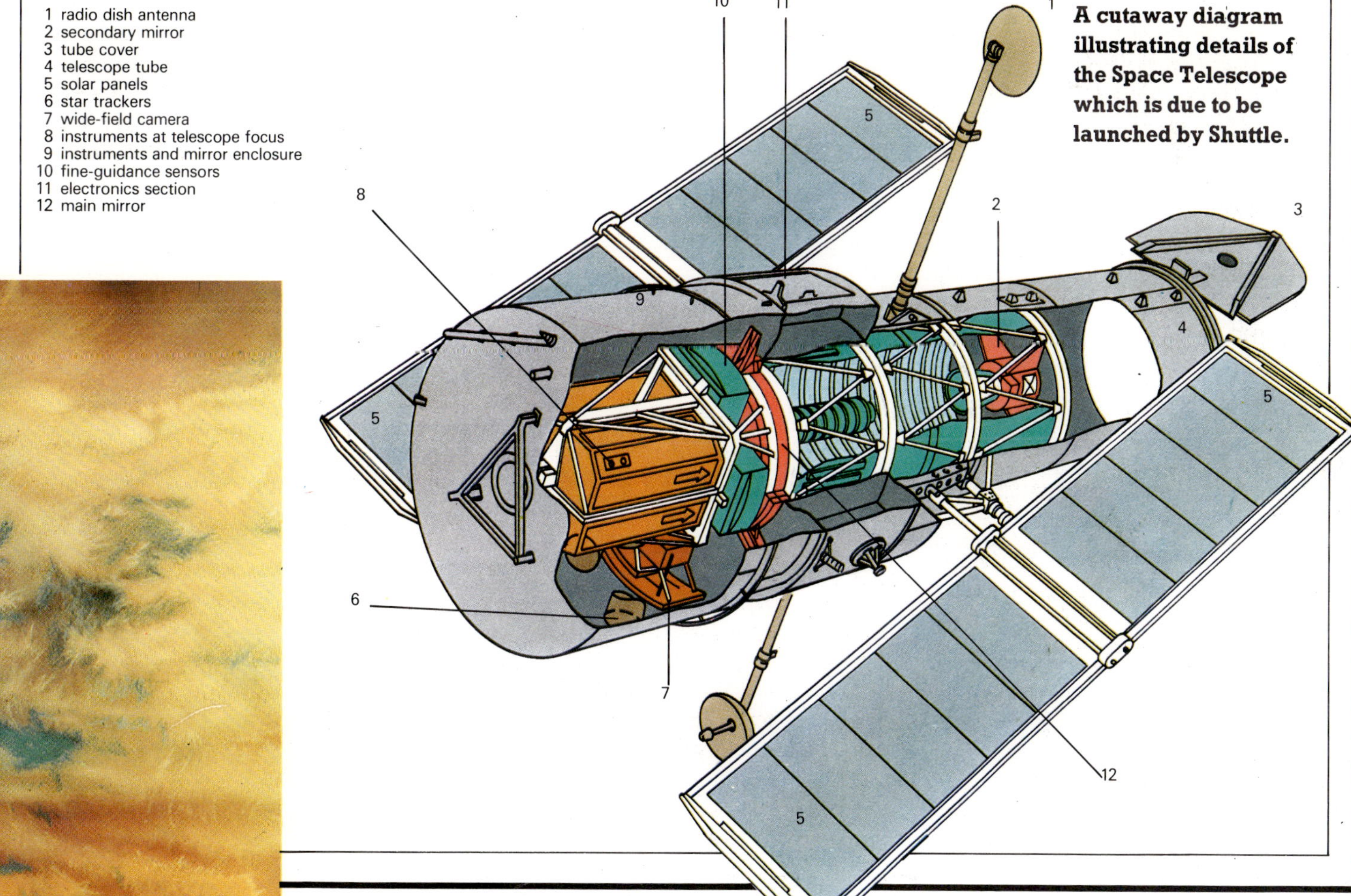

The Space Telescope

1 radio dish antenna
2 secondary mirror
3 tube cover
4 telescope tube
5 solar panels
6 star trackers
7 wide-field camera
8 instruments at telescope focus
9 instruments and mirror enclosure
10 fine-guidance sensors
11 electronics section
12 main mirror

A cutaway diagram illustrating details of the Space Telescope which is due to be launched by Shuttle.

NEXT IN SPACE

Both Russian and American space research is looking towards the development of permanent stations in space. To achieve this the stations would have to be fabricated from smaller units ferried up from the Earth's surface and assembled in space. Several of the *Shuttle* missions have included experiments into the feasibility of construction work in space.

A large permanent space station would give the opportunity to set up zero gravity and high vacuum factories, to become a base station for the assembly of deep space probes and to make long term scientific experiments possible.

MIR

On 20 February 1986 the USSR launched a new and important space vehicle. Called *Mir* (which means peace), the space vehicle is the primary building block for much larger space stations than the *Salyut* series of vehicles. *Mir* has six docking ports to which different laboratory, production and dwelling modules can be attached.

As is now the normal practice for Soviet launches, the vehicle is unmanned and will only be occupied after thorough tests have been completed on all its systems. Over the next three years modules will be gradually added to the basic vehicle. These modules include a technical workshop, astronomical laboratory, biological research laboratory and a drugs manufacturing module.

The *Mir* space station is a vital stage in the USSR's programme for a manned landing on Mars in the not too distant future.

NASA SPACE STATION

The American programme for the development of a space station is based on the use of the *Shuttle* craft as the main support vehicle with a larger unmanned cargo-carrying vehicle to bring up massive and

bulky objects.

Building in the zero gravity of space allows for much lighter and flimsier-looking structures than are possible on Earth. Modules and laboratories can be placed where needed in the structure.

Development work is now under way on a larger and improved version of the *Shuttle* craft to supply the station, and possibly take fare-paying passengers into space.

HOTOL

The British Aerospace *HOTOL* is a design for new generations of space craft. The *HOTOL* (horizontal take off and landing) space vehicle is designed to be much more like an aeroplane than earlier space craft. It would take off horizontally like a normal aeroplane but would leave its main undercarriage on the ground as it took off. Powered by a new type of rocket engine, which

would be able to take the oxygen it needed to burn its fuel directly from the atmosphere, the *HOTOL* would climb rapidly to the top of the atmosphere. At this point, with no more atmospheric oxygen available, it would switch over to a small tank of liquid oxygen to power it into orbit.

Like the *Shuttle* the *HOTOL* would then return to Earth using its wings like an aeroplane, but unlike the *Shuttle* it would be able to use its engines to make a powered descent—finally landing on its second undercarriage just like a normal aeroplane.

The *HOTOL* would be much larger than the current *Shuttle*, much safer and more economical. At the moment it is only in the initial development stages. *HOTOL* might also be developed into a super-fast airliner to replace *Concorde*, offering a journey time from London to Sydney of less than one hour!

Above: An artist's impression of the British Aerospace proposed space shuttle the HOTOL. It represents the next generation of space craft.

STARSHIPS

Space vehicles starting their journey from an orbiting space station could use rocket engines with much less thrust than is needed to escape the gravitational pull of the Earth. Instead of bulky chemical fuels, nuclear fusion could be used to eject a stream of high speed particles and propel the craft on its journey. Although acceleration would be slow the craft would eventually reach the very high speeds needed to cross the enormous distances between the stars. Several theoretical designs exist for engines of this type and in the future deep space probes may eventually be launched using them.

Above: This design for a space station is one of many under consideration by NASA. The Shuttle orbiter is shown docked with a factory module. At the bottom of the picture is a new design of unmanned cargo ferry for large loads.

CHAPTER 7

RECORD BREAKERS

Supermachines that break records are helping to test man's abilities to the limits. Successes and failures alike teach us more about the world we live in and about the materials and techniques we use. Although sport may seem to be a frivolous area to concentrate expensive effort on, all the improvements, that give that fine edge over the competition, are eventually incorporated into everyday machines.

Above all, the record breakers allow man to exercise his imagination and creative ability more freely. No one knows what might come out of this research in the future.

Man-powered flight and deep sea diving vessels aid research into unexplored areas.

Right: Ex World Champion Nikki Lauder gained more championship points than any other driver in his career. He is seen here, in his last season before retiring (1985), driving the highly successful McLaren Formula 1 racing car.

Marlboro
Marlboro
Marlboro
ALMA
ALMA
Marlboro
1
Shell
Shell

From the earliest days of motoring, attempts have been made to break the world land speed record. In the early days the same cars that were used for road racing were used in world record attempts.

Any reasonably flat surface such as a beach would be used for the attempt and speeds were well below 160 km/h (100 mph).

In 1907 Frederick Marriott raised the record to 257.5 km/h (150 mph) at Ormond Beach, Florida in the steam powered Stanley car, *Wogglebug*.

After this speeds increased and cars were specially built for record attempts. The surface on which the attempt was made had to be longer and completely smooth. Immense salt flats and dry lakes became the popular venues for attempts.

The record became standardized to the average speed, over a measured mile (1.609 km), on two runs in opposite directions, completed within strict time limits. These rules eliminated any advantage due to wind or land slope.

The vehicles used for record attempts bear little resemblance to the motor cars driven on the road. Engines have the same jets, or even rockets, used to power aircraft. Steering is precise but designed only to keep the car in a straight line.

Separate records now exist for vehicles driven by their own wheels and those directly powered by jet or rocket thrust. Classes also exist for different types of engine and for motorcycles.

Attempts are usually only made in a short season when the track and weather conditions are expected to be at their best. The record-attempting car, and a large group of support vehicles, are transported to the surface and the measured mile is marked out. A line is laid down for the driver to follow and official timekeepers take up position.

The car can take any length of run to pick up speed before entering the measured mile. At today's speeds this mile is completed in under five seconds. Parachutes are used to help slow down the vehicle before it stops and the car is quickly prepared for the return run.

Commercial sponsorship usually pays for record attempts.

In 1947 John Cobb took the land speed record at 634 km/h (394 mph) with the *Mobil Railton Special* which used aero engines to drive the wheels. This record stood for 16 years until the three wheel *Spirit of America*, which was powered directly by a jet engine, took the record for Craig Breedlove at 656 km/h (407 mph). Drivers of conventional vehicles protested that this car was really an aeroplane without wings and a separate class was eventually drawn up.

In 1965 Bob Summers' car *Goldenrod* set a record of 673 km/h (418 mph). Driven by four standard *Chrysler* car engines, this record still represents the ultimate achievement of the piston engine.

The current absolute world land speed record is held by Englishman Richard Noble in his jet propelled car *Thrust 2*, although this record is challenged by the unofficial record set up by Stan Barrett in the *Budweiser Rocket* over only one run.

Above: The rocket powered tricycle *Budweiser Rocket* broke the speed of sound in a land speed record attempt made in 1979.

Fact file . . .

The official world land speed record is 1019.467 km/h (633.468 mph) set by Richard Noble in *Thrust 2* on 4 October 1983 over the Black Rock Desert, Nevada. The highest peak land speed is 1190.377 km/h (739.666 mph) achieved by Stan Barrett in the *Budweiser Rocket* at Edwards Air Force Base in 1979.

Left: Richard Noble's world record breaking car *Thrust 2* using parachutes to slow down after a successful run. The car is powered by a jet engine taken from a Lightning fighter and can reach a speed of 163 km/h (100 mph) in under three seconds.

Left: The Class 1 catamaran power boat *Satisfaction* which won the American Benihana Offshore Grand Prix in 1981.

Below: Jockeying for position during the Class Formula IV NE mono-hull boat race at the Bristol docks.

Man's desire to travel at high speed extends also to travel on water. Powerboat racing is a fast and spectacular sport whether at sea or on inland water.

Water speed records are pursued with the same intensity as those on land.

Water sport has an added dimension to land sport as the surface conditions are subject to much greater variation—from flat and mirror like conditions to high waves in gales and storms.

OFFSHORE POWERBOAT RACING

Offshore powerboat racing is organized on several levels and with many different types of boat. The smallest class is the 2.4 metre (8 ft) junior class and the largest is the 18.3 metre (60 ft) Class 1 catamarans.

One of the classic races of the Class 1 season is the British Cowes-Torquay-Cowes 396 km (246 miles) race which is held annually in August. Conditions can be extremely variable. In calm conditions average speeds up to 127 km/h (79 mph) and maximum speeds of up to 160 km/h (100 mph) can be achieved. In rough conditions, with boats leaping out of the water, average speeds may only reach 77.9 km/h (48 mph).

Off Cowes, waves of up to 3 metres (10 ft) are possible. Drivers have to be extremely careful not to lift too high, or dive into the next wave and risk a disastrous 'flip'. In the 1981 race only four out of twelve starters finished the race.

The strain and shocks experienced by the crew are extremely intense and broken ankles are not uncommon. Careful attention must be paid to the suspension of the seats and to the strapping-in of the crew. Fire is also an ever present danger as large amounts of highly flammable fuel are carried.

Class 1 powerboats are extremely expensive to build and to support; a team of mechanics and a large road transporter are required. Leading entrants in the Class 1 World Championship are sponsored by major manufacturing companies.

Circuit racing, which takes place on rivers or lakes, is divided into races between hydroplanes and races between sports boats. The hydroplane classes are subdivided by engine type and capacity. Races are around a circuit of marker buoys over a number of laps.

The fastest class of boats in circuit racing is the OZ class. These boats have a maximum speed of about 210 km/h (130 mph). The boats usually have a catamaran hull which lifts out of the water at speed to ride on the very tips of the hulls. The hulls plane (skim) the surface of the water and the process is known as hydroplaning. This reduces water drag and increases speed but makes the boat more unstable. Wind can lift the nose of the boat and cause it to flip over. Engines on boats in this class are over 2000 cc capacity.

Many other hull forms are used in power boat racing. Boats that rise

Above: Dramatic pictures of the somersaulting *Bluebird K7* in which Donald Campbell was killed in January 1967 while attempting to raise the world speed record to over 483 km/h (300 mph).

Above: Tony Fahey's reversed three-pointer, jet propelled boat in which he hopes to capture the world speed record. The three ski-like contact areas which skim the water surface can be clearly seen.

up to ride on three hull points have come to be simply called hydroplanes. Two forward planing points at the end of sponsons (booms) support the front of the vessel and the third planing point is at the rear of the hull. The three-pointer, as it is also called, has minimum contact with the water, and in fact is lifted by air trapped underneath the main section of the hull—reducing water drag even further.

Other hull shapes include deep vee (a traditional monohull), cathedral (a triple hull type), and the vortex (a monohull with trailing outer hulls which increase stability).

Special classes exist for traditional monohulled power boats and for standard commercially available sports power boats.

Racing takes place in locations such as Bristol Docks in the UK, the Seine River in Paris, France, and Lake Como in Italy.

The world's first 'powerboat' was built in 1886 by Gottlieb Daimler—it reached a maximum speed of 10 km/h (6 mph).

By 1912 the powered water speed record had been raised to 74.8 km/h (46.51 mph) by Sir E. Mackay Edgar's *Maple Leaf IV* which used a multi-stepped hull to raise the boat higher out of the water and reduce drag.

In 1915 *Miss Minneapolis*, powered by an aeroplane engine, gave the record to Chris Smith with a speed of 107.28 km/h (66.66 mph). By the outbreak of World War II, Sir Malcolm Campbell had raised the record to 228.10 km/h (141.74 mph).

The craft used by Campbell was a three-pointer which was based on a design by the American Adolf E. Apel. Like all Campbell's boats and land-speed-record attempting cars the boat was called *Bluebird*; this one was *Bluebird K4*.

After the war Campbell fitted his boat with a de Havilland Goblin II jet engine to replace the Rolls-Royce piston engine he had used previously. The experiment was a failure as the boat proved too unstable.

In America the inaptly named *Slo Mo Shun IV* raised the record to 258.01 km/h (160 mph). The designer Ted Jones had discovered that at speeds above 240 km/h (150 mph) the boat would lift out of the water at the stern and the propeller would half rise out of the water. This reduced drag even further. The first prop-rider had been produced.

Slo Mo Shun further raised the record to 286.26 km/h (178 mph) and in 1962 *Miss US1* reached 322.419 km/h (200.419 mph).

Meanwhile Donald Campbell, the son of Sir Malcolm, had been working on similar ideas, but went on to build a new jet powered boat *Bluebird K7* which reached 325.6 km/h (202.32 mph) in 1955.

By 1964 he had raised the record to 444.6 km/h (276.33 mph). Having completed one run at 480 km/h (297 mph) in January 1967, he was killed when his craft took off and somersaulted only yards short of a new record.

Several drivers have been killed in attempts to break the water speed record over the years, including Sir Henry Segrave, John Cobb and Lee Taylor—illustrating the dangerous nature of attempts at this record.

The current record is held by Ken Warby in his boat *Spirit of Australia* with a speed of 514.389 km/h (319.627 mph) set 8 October 1978.

The ultimate test of the development of cars is the racetrack. Here engines, steering, brakes and chassis are all tested to breaking point.

The ultimate racetrack is that used by Formula 1 racing cars.

The drivers of Formula 1 cars are a very select group of people. Less than thirty cars can take part in most grand prix races. Only those drivers who have demonstrated exceptional driving skills in other classes of car racing will get a chance to race.

The best drivers are selected by the top racing teams to drive their very expensive Formula 1 cars. Most of the teams enter two cars and two drivers in the championship races.

The 'formula' of Formula 1 racing changes in some details each year to ensure that new cars will be developed and particular aspects of cars are tested further.

The dimensions, weight, fuel load and engine size are among the many details that are defined by the formula. Over the many years that grand prix races have been held a number of different formulas have been used with larger or smaller engine sizes.

For many years Formula 1 racing was dominated by three litre V-8 Ford Cosworth engined cars. Some years ago manufacturers were allowed to choose between the use of standard three litre engines and one and a half litre turbocharged engines.

The first of these turbocharged engines were unreliable and hungry for fuel. At first cars were allowed to refuel when necessary. This was considered to be a dangerous procedure and in the next season no refuelling was allowed and a maximum size of fuel tank was imposed.

Competitors soon learnt that by cooling the fuel before the race, more could be put into the tank.

This practice was then forbidden because of the danger of fuel expanding, if the start of the race was delayed.

Limits were placed on the total volume of fuel carried by the cars. Manufacturers were forced to make their cars more economical to run. For the 1986 season the fuel allowance was reduced by a further 12%—demanding even better fuel management.

Teams have gained temporary advantages by developing new techniques such as aerofoils and ground effect skirts to increase grip on corners and thus increase speeds. The other teams soon learn to copy any good idea that is allowed by the rules. All cars are carefully scrutinized both before and after races and any car that does not meet the very strict rules is disqualified.

Tyres are very important to the performance of grand prix cars. 'Slicks' are used which have no tread and gain grip by sticking to the track. As the tyres heat up the surface melts and becomes sticky. Different tyre compounds are used for different track and weather conditions: if the tyre is too soft it will wear out too quickly; if it is too hard it will not offer enough grip.

Two or three sets of tyres will be used in a 400 km (248 miles) race and the wrong choice can lose the race. There is a battle for grand prix dominance between various tyre manufacturers. To gain the advantage of starting at the front of the line up grid teams use special, extra soft, qualifying tyres, and specially tuned engines to obtain the fastest practice lap times.

A turbocharger increases the pressure of air flowing into the engine which in turn allows more fuel to be burned creating more power. The 'turbo' is driven by exhaust gases from the engine. The turbocharged engines produce up to 450 kw (603 hp) of power.

Modern Formula 1 cars have little suspension and a typical two hour long race tests both the car and the driver to the limit. The driver will have to change gear possibly every second of that time, and at speeds of up to 322 km/h (200 mph) concentration cannot lapse even for a split second.

Grand prix are won not only by speed but also by reliability. Often less than half of the cars that start a race will finish it. During the racing season grand prix teams travel around the various circuits like a great and colourful circus. Large trucks full of cars and engines or tyres draw up in the pits area. Tent awnings are put out to cover the cars. Large teams of mechanics arrive and set about preparing the cars for the race. Each team will probably prepare three cars—one as a spare in case either of the drivers' cars breaks down.

Practice engines are fitted and the first set of tyres put on. As engines are tuned the noise from the pit is deafening. The car for each driver is tailored to fit him; the seat is moulded to his body shape and pedals set to suit him.

There are two championships at stake—the drivers', which is won by the driver with the most points in the season, and the manufacturers', which is won by the team having the highest number of points for both their cars. There is often intense rivalry, even between drivers on the same team.

The eventual result of Formula 1 racing is the improvement of engine design and efficiency, safety and fuel economy on the standard saloon car. Already, many turbocharged standard cars are on the market. Formula 1 racing is at the forefront of Supermachine technology. It is a massively expensive sport which depends on sponsorship for its survival.

Left: The turbocharger on this BMW engine car has just failed and spilled fuel has caught fire. Grand Prix racing is highly dangerous and special fire fighting teams are placed around the circuit to deal with emergencies such as this.

Below: The Marlboro McLaren car driven here by Alain Prost during the 1985 season.

CHANNEL CROSSERS

In 1977, Bryan Allen, a cyclist, completed an aviation first and won a prize of £50,000 for the designers of his aircraft. The *Gossamer Condor* had completed a figure of eight course with turning points 805 metres (0.5 mile) apart. The 'first' was that the aircraft flown by Allen was pedal powered.

Man has attempted to fly under his own power since early historical times. At times the achievement was thought to be impossible because of the much more limited muscle power to weight ratio of a man when compared to that of a bird or bat.

Flight has been made possible by careful design of the aircraft and by the availability of lightweight materials for the construction.

The peak power available from a human power source is about 1.4 kw (1.89 hp), but only for short periods and with the use of both hands and feet.

The design for a man-powered aircraft must be as large and as light as possible. Several serious attempts were made in the 1960s to produce man-powered flying machines and several had some limited success.

EARLY FLIGHTS

The first truly man-powered aircraft, *Sumpac*, took to the air in 1961 from Hampshire. The aircraft was built at Southampton University.

Puffin 1 was built from spruce and balsa wood. Its planned weight was 34.1 kg (75 lb) but its actual weight was 50 kg (110 lb), mainly due to excessive glue absorption. Many design problems were encountered with *Puffin 1*, particularly with the balsa wood skin.

As a result of the problems with *Puffin 1*, *Puffin 2* employed a totally different wing structure with a skin of Melinex plastic. The structure was extremely tough but the weight was increased by 8.7 kg (19 lb). However, the performance of the aircraft was good enough to allow a flight of 908 m (993 yds) in 1962.

Jupiter was built in a similar manner to the *Puffins*. It had a 24 m (79 ft) long wing which itself weighed 41.8 kg (92 lb). The aerodynamic lift was excellent and in 1972 *Jupiter* established a distance record of 1.07 km (0.625 mile). Unfortunately, like all the early man-powered aircraft, it had poor directional control despite the tail mounted rudder.

These early aircraft were much too heavy to fly around the course specified for the Kremer £50,000 prize. It was thought that the prize would never be claimed.

THE CONDOR

Dr Paul MacCready and Dr Peter Lissaman from California decided that a large, light slow-flying vehicle

Left: The *Solar Challenger*, which is powered by an array of solar power cells which drive an electric motor, successfully crossed the channel in 1981.

Above: Bryan Allen in the cockpit of the *Gossamer Albatross*. An almost standard bicycle frame is used to pedal the aircraft into the sky.

Above: The *Gossamer Albatross* making its historic channel crossing. The *Albatross* flies tail first with a pusher propeller. The aircraft could only fly on a very calm and dry day.

was the answer and set about designing the *Gossamer Condor*.

To simplify development no radically new design features were incorporated. The *Condor* went through nine major design changes and suffered several crashes before it made the first man-powered flight of over a mile (1.6 km).

Standard bicycle pedals, sprockets and cranks were used to transmit the power to a propeller. Leading edges were made from corrugated cardboard and piano wire was used for bracing.

The wing shape was designed with the aid of a computer. The airframe was covered with an extremely lightweight plastic— transparent Mylar. No unnecessary additions were made to the bare minimum needed to fly the aircraft.

The *Condor* was a great success

and led to the development and construction of the *Gossamer Albatross*.

The *Albatross* was again flown by Bryan Allen and on 12 July 1979 it made an historic flight across the English Channel from Folkestone to Calais.

Bryan Allen's pedalling slowly rotated the large propeller. The *Albatross* was so well designed that for most of the flight Allen only had to supply 0.26 kw (0.35 hp) of power with occasional bursts of 0.9 kw (1.2 hp).

He was able to check his height above the channel by the use of an altimeter that had been adapted from the automatic focus mechanism of a Polaroid camera. A small propeller attached to the bowsprit (spine) of the aircraft indicated the air speed and allowed him to adjust his pedalling.

Extensive use was made of carbon fibre reinforced plastic in the construction of the *Albatross*. The wing ribs were cut from expanded polystyrene to keep their weight down to just 57 grammes.

Fact file . . .

The world distance record for man powered flight is held by Bryan Allen flying *Gossamer Albatross* on 12 June 1979 between England and France in 2 hours 49 minutes. The world distance record for solar powered flight is held by Steve Ptacek piloting *Solar Challenger* over 262.3 km (163 miles).

TO THE OCEAN BED

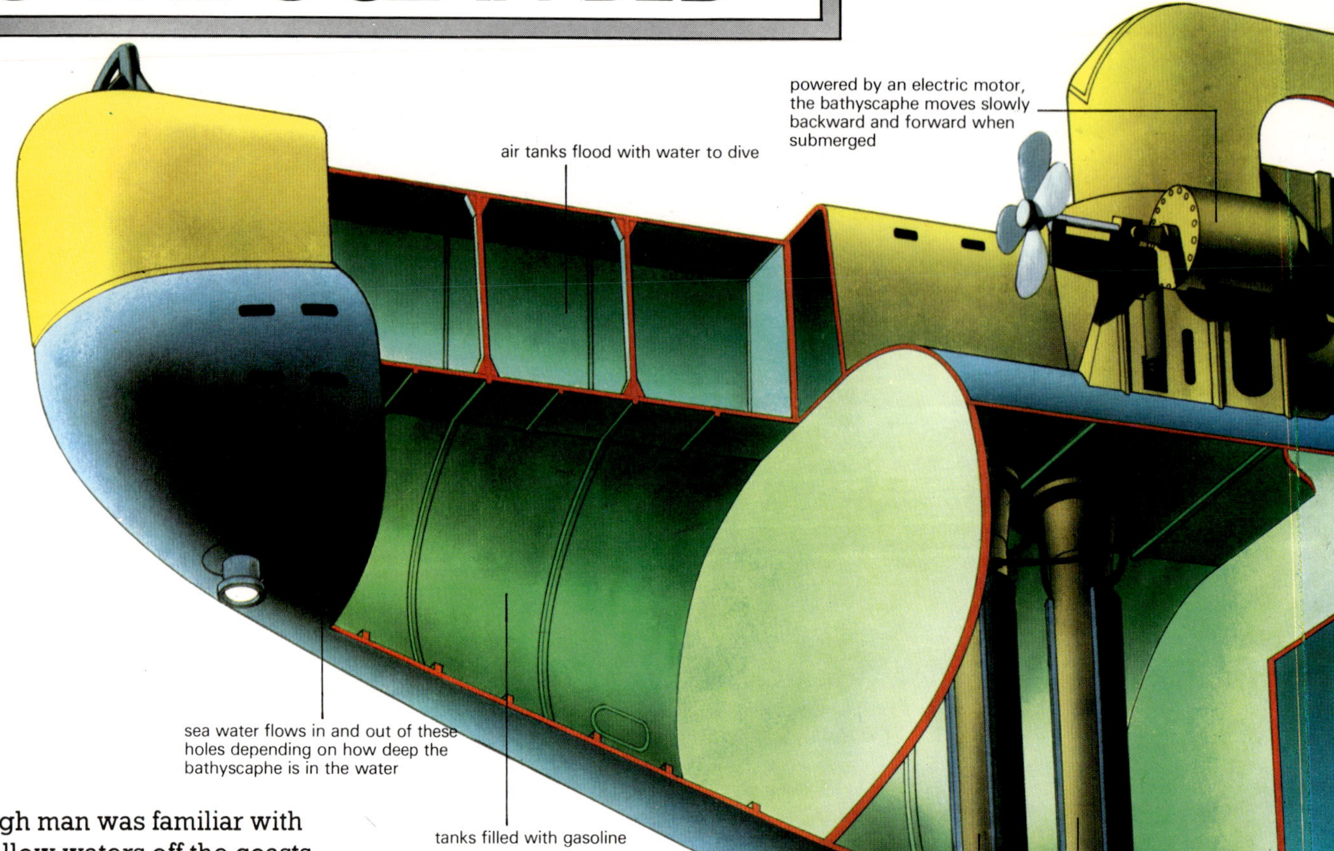

Although man was familiar with the shallow waters off the coasts of most countries, the ocean depths remained a mystery until well into the 20th century.

The pressure of water increases rapidly with increasing depth: unprotected divers could only dive to about 50 metres (165 ft).

A protective vessel would be needed to allow man to dive to the much greater depths that he knew were there. In 1930 two Americans, William Beebe and Otis Barton, designed the *Bathysphere*.

Between 1930 and 1934 Beebe and Barton carried out a series of dives in the Caribbean Sea. They were the first humans to see the underwater world below 300 metres (1000 ft), although it was so dark that little, in fact, could be seen. They also made a record breaking descent to 923 metres (3028 ft).

The *Bathysphere* was a 1.5 metre (5 ft) diameter sphere which was lowered on a steel cable from a boat. This prevented any free exploration when the *Bathysphere* was submerged. The sphere had three tiny portholes made of quartz. A telephone line was used to communicate with the surface.

A few years after the pioneering work of Beebe and Barton, Professor Auguste Piccard from Switzerland designed the *Bathyscape*. The name in Greek means deep-ship. Like the *Bathysphere* the crew compartment was a metal sphere but this was attached to a massive float. The *Bathyscape* did not need to be attached to a ship and had propellers to allow it to explore the ocean depths.

The inside diameter of the crew sphere was 2 metres (6.5 ft) with walls 9 centimetres (3.5 inches) thick. Once the crew were aboard air tanks in the float were flooded with water causing the vessel to sink. As the vessel continued its descent water entered the gasoline tanks to prevent the increasing water pressure from crushing the float. More water entered as the gasoline cooled and contracted and the vessel continued to dive. To slow the dive down the crew could release iron pellets which were carried as ballast.

Underneath the vessel a heavy chain would hit the sea bed and cause the vessel to hover just above the bottom. Powerful lights were then used to illuminate the sea bed around the vessel. To return to the surface iron pellets were released.

the vessel in 1958 and it was taken to California. A new cabin was fitted and a new series of dives started.

On 23 January 1960, Dr Jaques Piccard, the inventor's son, and Lt. Donald Walsh of the U.S. Navy went to the bottom of the Marianas Trench in the Pacific Ocean. They reached a depth of 10,912 metres (35,802 ft). The pressure at that depth was 1100 times greater than at the surface of the sea.

The Bathyscape deep sea exploration vehicle still holds the record for the deepest dive into the oceans. Modern deep sea vessels often incorporate robot arms to help lift objects off the sea bed.

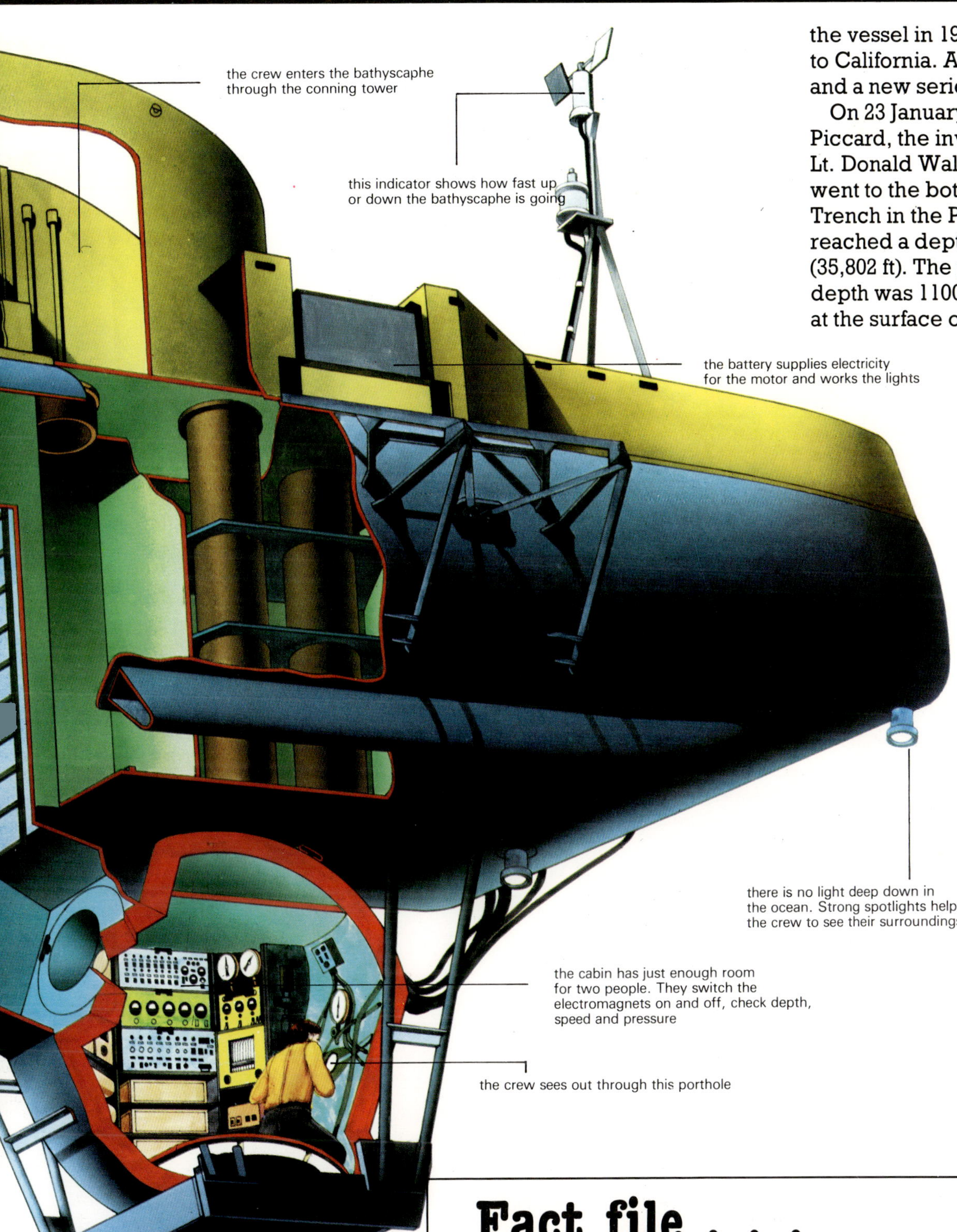

The *Bathyscape* was first tested off the coast of West Africa in 1948. Professor Piccard went down to a depth of over 3 km (2 miles) in a second version of the craft which was called the *Trieste*.

The United States Navy took over

Fact file . . .

The record-breaking descent into the Marianas Trench took 4 hours 48 minutes and the return to the surface took 3 hours 17 minutes.

The greatest depth from which an object has been salvaged is 5,029 m (16,500 ft), by the Bathyscape *Trieste II* in 1972.

INDEX